URANIA

Da Capo Press Music Reprint Series

URANIA

A Choice Collection of Psalm-Tunes, Anthems, and Hymns

By James Lyon

New preface by Richard Crawford, *University of Michigan*

DA CAPO PRESS · NEW YORK · 1974

Library of Congress Cataloging in Publication Data

Lyon, James, 1735-1794, comp.
  Urania.

  (Da Capo Press music reprint series)
  Reprint of the 1761 ed.
  Includes bibliographies.
  1. Tune-books. 2. Hymns, English. 3. Anthems. I. Title.
M2116.L99 1974   783-9'52   69-11667
ISBN 0-306-71198-2

Copyright © 1974 by Da Capo Press, Inc.
A Subsidiary of Plenum Publishing Corporation
227 West 17th Street, New York, New York 10011

PREFACE

When, in 1764, Josiah Flagg (1737–c.1795) of Boston brought out his *Collection of the Best Psalm Tunes*, he apologized in his preface for offering a new collection "at a time when there are already so many among us." Since only a handful of American tune collections predate Flagg's, most of them pamphlets much smaller than his work, Flagg's apology can be taken as proof that his collection was issued to compete in the market with foreign publications. Fortunately, Flagg chose to enumerate some of his competitors by citing the sources of many of his tunes. Arnold, Williams, Tans'ur, Ashworth, Adams, and Davenport make up a list of British psalmodists whose works, already available to Americans by the 1760's, served Flagg and later American compilers as models and musical sources through the rest of the century. But in his list, Flagg does not stop with the names of British compilers; he goes on to include an American: James Lyon, whose *Urania* had appeared in Philadelphia in 1761.

The year before *Urania* was published, Lyon had advertised it accurately as "the first Attempt of the kind to spread the Art of Psalmody, in its Perfection, thro' our American Colonies."[1]

Urania was much larger than any of its American predecessors; it was the first collection set primarily for four voices, rather than two or three; it was the first to identify new (*i.e.*, American) compositions; it was the first to carry "fuging-tunes," and with its ample selection of anthems and hymns, the first to contain music other than psalm tunes. The innovations are impressive, yet the uniqueness of Lyon's collection should not be overemphasized. For while many things about *Urania* were new to the field of American musical publication, they were not new to the tradition in which it was rooted—the tradition of Anglo-American psalmody. Josiah Flagg's recognition of Lyon's collection points to its greatest significance: *Urania* is the first American collection of sacred music whose size and repertory make it worthy to take a place alongside the estimable British collections on which it was based.

* * * *

James Lyon was born in Newark, New Jersey, in 1735, and earned an A.B. degree from the College of New Jersey

i

(Princeton) in 1759. Two years later he published *Urania* in Philadelphia. Lyon's alma mater granted him an M.A. degree in 1762, and the Presbyterian Synod of New Brunswick, New Jersey, licensed him to preach. Ordained by his church in 1764, he was sent to Nova Scotia. In 1772 he accepted a call to become minister at Machias, a settlement far up the coast of eastern Maine. Lyon served as pastor at Machias for most of his remaining years, though he left briefly in 1773 and again during the period 1783–85. He died in 1794.[2]

A good deal of information survives about certain periods of James Lyon's life, but nothing has been discovered of his musical background or training. The earliest known mention of Lyon as a musician dates from 1759, when a composition of his was performed at his commencement from the College of New Jersey (Sonneck, p. 124–27). He seems to have taught a singing-school in Philadelphia after his graduation (p. 127–28), and by May of 1760 the music for *Urania* was compiled and ready to be engraved (p. 135). Lyon apparently continued his singing-school in the fall of 1760 (p. 127–28), he composed music for the commencement at the College of Philadelphia in May of the next year (p. 128), saw *Urania* through the press (p. 135–36), and presented more of his own music during the ceremony at which he received his Master's degree in September, 1762 (p. 129).

That year, Lyon's twenty-eighth, marks a turning point in his life. His licensing as a clergyman apparently brought to an end his professional involvement in music, and from 1762 until his death he pursued what Sonneck refers to as an "erratic but uncommonly interesting clerical and political career" (p. 132).

Yet an entry in an acquaintance's diary for April, 1774, demonstrates Lyon's musical reputation at that time, and describes his musical skill and continued commitment to his art:

> [April 22] I met with that great master of music, Mr. Lyon. He sung at my request, & sings with his usual softness and accuracy. He is about publishing a new Book of Tunes which are to be chiefly of his own Composition. . . . [April 23] At home drawing off some of Mr. Lyon's Tunes . . . Afternoon according to Appointment I visited Mr. Lyon at Mr. Hunters. He sings with great accuracy. I sung with him many of his Tunes & had much conversation on music. He is vastly fond of music & musical genius's. We spent the Evening with great satisfaction to me.[3]

Lyon's "new Book of Tunes" was never published. But during the 1770's and 1780's new compositions from his pen occasionally appeared in American tunebooks, indicating that he maintained contact with active musicians.

One might infer from *Urania*—from the boldness of its conception and its list of distinguished subscribers—that James Lyon was an unusually adventurous, determined man. That inference is supported by what is known about his later career. Much of what Lyon did during the last thirty years of his life was determined by the environment in which he chose to spend them: the northern country of Nova Scotia and eastern Maine. His removal from Philadelphia and Princeton, where there is every indication that he flourished, to Nova Scotia may seem puzzling, but it becomes less so when it is known that Philadelphia land companies actively promoted the settlement of Nova Scotia in the early 1760's.[4] In the wake of a long conflict for North American possessions, the British had routed the French from that territory, and settlers from the British Isles and the Colonies arrived to take their places. The newly-ordained Lyon went north to fill their need for a clergyman.

From the very beginning of his stay in Nova Scotia Lyon's interest seems to have extended beyond the spiritual affairs of his flock to the land itself. In April of 1765, for example, he is named, together with a Philadelphia land company's organizer and its surveyor, as one of a three-man exploring party, ranging far from the central settlement near Pictou.[5] And years later, writing from Machias, he reminded his correspondent: "It is . . . well known, that I have explored Nova Scotia, in almost every part," and forwarded in the same letter a map of some three hundred miles of the Nova Scotian coastline, with the assurance that it was "very accurate."[6] At the beginning of the War for Independence Lyon even went so far as to propose by letter to George Washington that he, Lyon, lead an expedition to wrest Nova Scotia from British hands. He offered himself as leader, he explained, because he knew the land so well.[7] Lyon's proposal demonstrates both his attachment to the country in which he spent his first pastorate and his tendency to involve himself in matters not directly related to his clerical calling.

When Lyon accepted the call to become pastor at Machias in 1772, the town fathers offered the hope that they could "provide for his Comfortable Support, that temporal Cares may not perplex and divide his time."[8] The hope was a vain one. Within three years the war against Great Britain had broken out. Threatened by the British, Machias formed a Committee of Safety and Correspondence to deal with the danger, and, far from shunning "temporal cares," Lyon took them directly upon himself by becoming chairman of the Committee. In his role as chairman he corresponded with the Massachusetts legislature (Maine was a part of Massachusetts territory until early in the nineteenth century) over the next few years, reporting the heroic capture of an armed British ship by the men of Machias in 1775,[9] and complaining in 1776–77 about the growing privations suffered by Machias's citizens, and the lack of aid from their government in combating the isolated community's lack of provisions.[10] Lyon's own position as pastor and community leader had not spared him the difficulties which beset his people, and in 1777 he requested a small loan to buy utensils for a salt distillery he had begun to operate:

> I have been obliged to strain every nerve, even to the neglect of my proper agreeable business, in order to procure the bare necessaries of life. But through want of the proper means I have failed in a great measure, & have suffered much both in body & mind. My bread is Indian, procured with great difficulty; my drink water, my meat moose, & my clothing rags, & many of these the dear partner of my misfortunes [Mrs. Lyon], who was tenderly educated has been obliged to beg from those who could illy spare them.[11]

Despite the hardships, however, Lyon, who one imagines could surely have moved to a less trying situation, elected to remain in Machias for most of the rest of his life.

Musician and composer, clergyman and author,[12] explorer, patriot, and distiller of salt, James Lyon possessed a rare combination of talent and resourcefulness. Indeed, he was the kind of man Americans like to think of as typically American. He was a man of many parts.

*   *   *   *

DESCRIPTION OF *URANIA*

Oscar Sonneck has solved many of the major questions about *Urania*'s bibliographical history in his monograph on Lyon (Chapter 2, p. 134–47). Using contemporaneous newspapers and the collection itself, of which he managed to examine and compare thirteen different copies, Sonneck discovered that Lyon had selected the music for *Urania* by the end of May, 1760, when he first advertised for subscribers. Though he announced that engraving would begin when he had received subscriptions for four hundred copies, he was apparently ready to proceed with half that number; a later advertisement indicates that the work was underway by mid-July, and the list printed in *Urania* shows that only two hundred and ten copies were subscribed. Sonneck presents evidence to show that *Urania* was completed and sent to subscribers before the end of 1761, that it was available to the public in June, 1762, and that it appeared in at least two later editions (Philadelphia, 1767, and New York, 1773), all three editions being identical in musical content. He also suggested that another edition may have been printed, "perhaps in New England," but was unable to find a reference to support that possibility.

The title page of *Urania*, the rules for singing, and the music were engraved on copper plate, leaving only the dedication, the index, and the list of subscribers to be set typographically. Sonneck's comparison of copies turned up no variations in engraved matter. But variations in the typeset pages led him to the conclusion that these were reset for each new printing. By meticulous comparison of the typographical matter, Sonneck arrived at a hypothesis which would cover the three editions whose appearance he could document from newspaper advertisements. The evidence he presents, however, indicates that *Urania* was printed not just three but at least five different times. Establishing the chronology of editions lies outside the scope of this study, although two general principles help to set guidelines. First, since there was no reason for a subscriber list to appear in later printings, copies which carry it must be first editions. Second, printing mistakes, of which *Urania* was not entirely free, provide another clue, for one can assume that uncorrected copies predate corrected ones. The reader may consult Appendix I for particulars on the six known printings. But more detailed bibliographical work will have to be done before the remaining questions about *Urania's* printing history can be settled.

Though the printer's name does not appear anywhere in *Urania*, and though Sonneck fails to identify him, there is no reason to dispute the traditional attribution to William Bradford (1722–1791),[13] which is supported by a good deal of circumstantial evidence. In Lyon's first advertisement for subscribers, he and Bradford are the only ones mentioned as taking subscriptions in Philadelphia. And when the work was announced as generally available to the public, it could be purchased from "Messrs. Rivington, Bradford and Isaac Snowden." While the list might look like a single company run by a triumvirate, it actually represents three separate firms. Of the three, only Bradford was operating a press at the time. When one adds to this evidence the fact that Bradford was himself a subscriber to *Urania* and that he printed in 1762 and 1763 two other pamphlets of music which almost surely were composed by Lyon, little doubt can remain that he also printed *Urania*.

The engraver of *Urania* was Henry Dawkins (fl. 1753–1780), whose name appears on the title page. A newspaper advertisement from 1758 describes Dawkins's accomplishments: "He engraves all sorts of maps, shopkeepers bills, bills of parcel, coats of arms, cyphers, and other devices on plate; likewise seals, and mourning rings cut after the neatest manner."[14] Music-engraving is not mentioned, nor is it likely that he tried his hand at it until Lyon hired him for *Urania*. Historians of American engraving do not rate Dawkins very highly as an artist, but he was equal to the task Lyon set for him. His work was far more skillful than any earlier American music engraver's, and it compares favorably in appearance with that of the best of the later ones.

The title page of *Urania* describes its content and purpose:

> Urania, or a choice collection of psalm-tunes, anthems, and hymns, from the most approv'd authors, with some entirely new; in two, three, and four parts. The whole peculiarly adapted to the use of churches, and private families: to which are prefix'd the plainest, & most necessary rules of psalmody.

As indicated, the musical portion of *Urania* begins with a selection of psalm-tunes—seventy of them, to be exact. It may seem curious that the psalm-tunes appeared without text, but the omission can be explained. Many different versifications of the psalms were circulating in America when *Urania* appeared, the most popular being Tate and Brady's *New Version of the Psalms of David* (London, 1696; reprinted often in both Great Britain and America), and Isaac Watts's *Psalms of David Imitated* (London, 1719; also reprinted often on both sides of the Atlantic). The textless tunes in *Urania* could be used equally well with any versification. Space may also have been a consideration. Most psalms run to several stanzas or more, and while the first could be set under the music, the others would have to be placed at the bottom of the page. Most contemporaneous English collections included several stanzas in that way, but then many of them, unlike *Urania*, were printed from type rather than engraved, and text engraved in Dawkins's cursive style was bound to occupy more space than text printed from type. (Lyon did supply text for his hymn-tunes because these texts were not available in the standard metrical psalters.)

The psalm-tunes in *Urania* are divided into two groups. The first, made up of thirty-eight nicknamed tunes (e.g., MEAR), is arranged by poetic meter: common-meter tunes appear first, then short-meter tunes and finally long-meter tunes.[15] The second group is made up of thirty-two "proper" tunes—compositions named for the particular psalm to which they are to be sung (e.g., PSALM 4). Following the psalm-tunes is a selection of anthems, the largest and most elaborate type of composition published by eighteenth-century American compilers. The dozen anthems in *Urania* vary somewhat among themselves, but generally they are through-composed settings of scriptural text, usually prose, with frequent repetition of words and phrases, and changes of choral texture.[16] *Urania* concludes with a group of fourteen hymn-tunes: settings of non-scriptural devotional poetry. Hymn-singing had been proscribed in early Calvinist worship, and not until nearly the middle of the eighteenth century did it become established as a worthy addition to psalm-singing. In line with the comparative novelty of hymnody in America, Lyon underlaid his hymn-tunes with texts.

Lyon's title page identifies the composers whose tunes he printed as "the most approved authors," and an examination of the music shows how broadly that designation could be stretched. The tunes in *Urania* were composed over a period of more than two centuries, and marked differences in musical style may be observed among them. Of the eighty-four psalm and hymn-tunes in Lyon's collection, seventeen were composed during the sixteenth and seventeenth centuries, for use with Sternhold and Hopkins's versification of the psalms, the so-called "Old Version," first published in London in 1562. Most of these tunes are plain and unadorned, moving in block chords with little melodic decoration, and displaying touches of modality in their harmonies (see WINDSOR, p. 3). Another sixteen tunes first appeared in print between 1700 and 1725, some as settings of hymns, and others as settings of psalms in Tate and Brady's *New Version*. This bloc of tunes tends, for the most part, to be slightly more embellished and more clearly tonal than the earlier group (see CROWLE, p. 7). An additional thirty-six tunes appeared after 1725. Most of the psalm-tunes among them are considerably more elaborate than those composed earlier. Not only are their melodic lines usually embellished with melismas; many display changes in texture, with sections set for only one or two voices alternating with full four-part choral sections (see DORCHESTER, p. 23). Imitation appears in some of the psalm-tunes as well, and several are examples of British "fuging-tunes" (see PSALM 12, p. 46).[17] The hymn-tunes among the group composed after 1725 are mostly embellished with grace-notes and display the melodic and harmonic idiom of solo songs (See KETTLEBY'S, p. 174).

With the exception of a single psalm-tune (PSALM 100 NEW) which appears to have originated in America, Lyon found all of the compositions mentioned so far in British sources. But he also identified four of his psalm and hymn-tunes as "entirely new"—never before published—indicating that they came either from his own pen or from that of another American composer.[18]

This survey has left unidentified the source of fifteen of Lyon's eighty-four psalm and hymn-tunes. Giovanni Palma (fl. c. 1760), a musician active in Philadelphia during the 1750's, composed one of the fifteen, and another immigrant professional, William Tuckey (1708–1781), seems to have provided two more. Stylistic evidence indicates that most if not all of the twelve remaining pieces are eighteenth-century compositions, and it seems likely that they will eventually be located through further examination of British collections.

Most of the twelve anthems which complete the musical portion of *Urania* were surely composed after 1725. Mid-eighteenth-century British sources contain seven, two are identified by Lyon as "new," another is the work of Tuckey, and the remaining two have not been traced.

The title page of *Urania* notes that the compositions are "in

Two, Three, and Four, Parts." Lyon is quite consistent here. All of the psalm-tunes and all but two of the anthems are set for four voices. The hymns, most of them set to decorated, wide-ranging melodies, are written for fewer voices than the psalm-tunes: seven for three voices and seven for two. Of the remaining anthems, one is composed for three voices and the other for two.

According to its title page *Urania* was "peculiarly adapted to the use of churches and private families." The latter seem an unlikely clientele for a volume as large, expensive, and musically diverse as *Urania*, and it is doubtful that many copies were sold for family use. Lyon seems to have made an effort to enlist clerical patronage for his collection by dedicating *Urania* "to the clergy of every denomination." It is difficult to know from a distance of two centuries whether he was successful in that attempt, but his roster of subscribers does list seventeen ministers among its one hundred forty-one names. A work like the *Collection of Psalm Tunes* which Francis Hopkinson[19] compiled in 1763 for Christ Church and St. Peter's Church in Philadelphia, a volume far smaller, less varied, and cheaper than *Urania*, would seem to be better suited to church use than Lyon's collection.

Lyon's title page does not mention another use to which *Urania* might have been put: it might have served as a singing-school textbook. Singing-schools had begun to be formed in America early in the eighteenth century in response to the desire of religious leaders to improve the quality of congregational singing by teaching people to read music. A typical school, taught by a singing-master who might himself be a composer, ran for about three months, with the scholars meeting two or three times a week, learning the fundamentals of note-reading and vocal production and perhaps presenting a public performance at the conclusion of the session. Since the avowed purpose of the school was to teach note-reading, the scholars sang from manuscript or printed music, and collections like *Urania* provided instructional material. Since Lyon himself apparently taught a singing-school in Philadelphia in 1759 and 1760, it is not at all unlikely that that experience led him to put together a collection of his own. Perhaps Lyon failed to mention singing-schools on his title page because he wished to emphasize that *Urania* was a devotional as well as a didactic aid, but the subsequent history of American psalmody makes it clear that tune-book sales were determined more by singing-schools and musical societies than by the church.

As the title page of *Urania* reports, to the large selection of compositions are "prefix'd the plainest, & most necessary rules of psalmody." Following the precedent set by earlier compilers, Lyon began his collection with a theoretical introduction, enhancing his work's instructional value. The introduction, which covers a dozen pages, concentrates almost entirely on explaining note-reading, with the last two-and-one-half pages presenting some exercises for beginning singers. Sonneck prints Lyon's introduction in full in his study of Lyon, and, having identified some of Lyon's theoretical sources, comes to the conclusion that the form and writing of the introduction were his own.[20]

There remains one more aspect of *Urania* to be described: Lyon's subscriber list, which would in itself serve as an interesting subject for an article. The list is especially valuable because all but fifty of the one hundred forty-one people on it are identified by something more than their names. Lyon's identifications show that his alma mater stood solidly in support of his endeavor. Two presidents (Samuel Davies died in 1761 and was replaced by Samuel Finley), the steward, and three tutors of the college appear as subscribers, as do ten graduates and twenty-two students enrolled at the time *Urania* appeared—a total of thirty-nine Princetonians. And though only one student from the College of Philadelphia subscribed, Lyon succeeded in gaining the support of the provost and vice-provost of that institution as well. Two more groups gave *Urania* substantial backing: merchants, of whom sixteen are listed, and clergy, thirteen of whom subscribed (not counting the four ministers who were college officials). The identifications of the rest of Lyon's subscribers are scattered. Three physicians and a military man appear, as do six men designated "Esquire," apparently in reference to their high standing in society. Finally, eleven subscribers are identified by their residences, which range from several in New England to New York, New Jersey, outstate Pennsylvania, Maryland, Virginia, and even a visitor from the West Indies. This list leaves fifty subscribers identified by name only, and in view of Lyon's carefully drawn categories, it can be inferred that the fifty—among whom nine were women—were not connected with either the College of New Jersey or the College of Philadelphia, were not merchants nor clergymen nor doctors nor soldiers nor "gentlemen," and that as of 1761 they were local residents, living in or near Princton or, more likely, Philadelphia.

Space will not permit anything more than the briefest comments on those whom Lyon enlisted to help him publish *Urania*. But it might be well to note that at least twenty-two achieved sufficient stature to earn their own entries in the *Dictionary of American Biography*. Some subscribers, like the college officials named, or like William Bradford, the printer of *Urania*, had already made important contributions. Others were to make their mark in later years: Rev. John Ewing (1732–1802), for example, who was to become provost of the University of Pennsylvania; James Manning (1738–1791), who helped found Rhode Island College (Brown University) and was its first president; Benjamin Rush (1745–1813), active as a patriot during the Revolution, who became the most important American physician and medical researcher of his time.[21]

The subscriber list of *Urania* provides a glimpse, albeit a brief and incomplete one, of the society into which *Urania* was issued. It shows that a relatively heterogeneous group of citizens mostly in and around Philadelphia—students and college presidents, preachers, women, and merchants—joined together to support the endeavor. But Lyon's list was not sufficiently heterogeneous to include the name of any known musician, and it is with a certain amount of puzzlement that one contemplates the absence of Francis Hopkinson, who, from the distance of two centuries, might seem *Urania's* most likely subscriber.

*   *   *   *

THE PEDIGREE OF *URANIA*

Many of the tunes James Lyon printed in *Urania* appeared in a variety of harmonizations in earlier collections; this is the chief difficulty in discovering Lyon's sources. Finding an earlier printing of a tune in *Urania* proves nothing unless all of the voices are similar to those in Lyon's printing—unless, in Sonneck's phrase, the *settings* of the tune "correspond convincingly" (p. 176). And only when the setting occurs in a collection roughly contemporaneous with *Urania* can that collection be claimed as the source. "Lyon probably knew such older standard compilations as, for instance, Ravenscroft's Whole Booke of Psalms," writes Sonneck, "but so did many other psalmodists who preceded Lyon. It would therefore be rather a delicate undertaking [read: 'It would be unwise'] to point to the 17th-century collections as sources of *Urania*" (p. 176n.). Of the ninety-six compositions in Lyon's collection, sixty-five have been discovered in earlier printings which correspond convincingly with the settings in *Urania*; ten more appear to be first printings; the melodies of thirteen more have been traced, but no setting which corresponds with Lyon's has been found; and finally, no earlier printings of the remaining eight have been located.

As Clarence Brigham and Irving Lowens have demonstrated, the title-page of *Urania*, with its border engraved in so-called Chippendale style, was accorded the ultimate eighteenth-century accolade: its design was copied and used for the title pages of two later American tunebooks, Josiah Flagg's *Collection of the Best Psalm Tunes* (1764), and Andrew Law's *Select Harmony* (1779).[22] It now can be deducted that *Urania*'s title-page was based on, though not literally copied from, *Harmonia Sacra*, a tune collection published in London by Thomas Butts.[23] (See Plate I.) The title page of *Harmonia Sacra*, signed "Morrison Sculpt. Moorfields," is far more elaborate than any similar production of eighteenth-century America, containing six musical angels within its Chippendale border. Henry Dawkins's *Urania* title page depicts only one, and consequently the resemblance may not be immediately apparent, though it should be noted that, like the figures in *Harmonia Sacra*, Dawkins's lady is seated on a cloud. But the decoration of the two titles is similar, *Urania*'s subtitle virtually duplicates Butts's, the breaking of lines is the same, and the specification of voice parts enclosed within a pair of extended lines is very similar. The differences that do exist are explained by the content of the two collections. There is no question that Lyon knew *Harmonia Sacra*; he borrowed seven tunes from it. And the musical portion of *Urania* shares with *Harmonia Sacra* a notational peculiarity that strengthens the link: half-note stems in both collections appear on the right-hand side of the note, no matter what its position on the staff. Thus, for example, Lyon prints the tune PUBLICK WORSHIP in a version identical with *Harmonia Sacra* in all three musical parts, and, with the exception of a few note stems in the melody (second and third phrases), identical in its engraving as well. (See Plate II. Cf. p. 178.) And if to the similarities noted here one adds the classical titles (only two other eighteenth-century American collections of sacred music bear a non-English title, and only a single non-English title besides *Harmonia Sacra* has been discovered among the more than one hundred British collections published between 1730 and 1760), one comes to the conclusion that the engraved title page of *Urania* was inspired by *Harmonia Sacra*.[24]

Though *Harmonia Sacra* was an important source for *Urania*,

Plate I. Title-page of *Harmonia Sacra*, London, c. 1760   Courtesy of The Library of Congress.

Plate II. "Publick Worship" from *Harmonia Sacra*. Courtesy of The Library of Congress.

Lyon drew a greater number of compositions from three other British collections: Caleb Ashworth's *Collection of Psalm Tunes* (London, c. 1760; 14 tunes), John Arnold's *Compleat Psalmodist* (4th edition, London, 1756; 12 tunes), and Abraham Adams's *Psalmodist's New Companion* (6th edition, London, c. 1760; 10 tunes). Similarities with all three extend beyond the repertory. Sonneck has demonstrated that Lyon based at least a part of his theoretical introduction on Arnold's work.[25] Adams's collection displays the same method of stemming half-notes as *Harmonia Sacra* and *Urania*. As for Ashworth's *Collection*, its format may have provided the model for the first section of *Urania*'s music. Unlike most British psalm-tune collections of the eighteenth century, Ashworth's is designed to accommodate itself to any collection of religious poetry: its tunes are textless, and it is arranged by meter rather than by psalm number or by whim. Like Ashworth, Lyon presented textless psalm-tunes and arranged them by meter.

An assortment of six different British collections provided the source for sixteen more tunes in *Urania*: Uriah Davenport's *Psalm-Singer's Pocket Companion* (London, 1755; 5 tunes), John Arnold's *Leicestershire Harmony* (London 1759; 4 tunes), *The Divine Musical Miscellany* (London, 1754; 2 tunes), Israel Holdroyd's *Spiritual-man's Companion* (5th edition, London, 1753; 2 tunes), John Smith's *Set of Services, Anthems & Psalm Tunes* (London, c. 1750; 2 tunes), and James Green's *Book of Psalmody* (8th edition, London, 1734; 1 tune).

Citing the ten British collections which served Lyon as sources does not complete the task of establishing the pedigree of *Urania*. For at least six separate tune collections, intended as supplements for metrical psalters, were published in America before Lyon's work appeared. The most important American psalter, the *Bay Psalm Book*, includes a small musical supplement in the ninth (Boston, 1698) and later editions. The tunes, however, were monophonic in almost all editions, and not until the twenty-fourth edition (Boston, 1737), with thirty-nine tunes set for three voices, did the *Bay Psalm Book* include an appreciable supplement of harmonized music. Meanwhile, John Tufts's *Introduction to the Singing of Psalm-Tunes* (Boston, 1721; no copy discovered), first issued with a group of monophonic tunes, appeared in 1723 with the music harmonized for two voices, and ran through six editions from 1726 to 1744 with a set of three-voice tunes; Thomas Walter's *Grounds and Rules of Musick* (Boston, 1721) carried a changing collection of tunes for three voices through some half-dozen separate editions before 1761; and a tune-supplement engraved by Thomas Johnston (Boston, 1755) appeared in at least two versions. Rounding out the list are two collections extant in a single edition only: a group of tunes engraved by James Turner (Boston, 1752), and William Dawson's *Youth's Entertaining Amusement* (Philadelphia, 1754).

Taken together, the American collections made available a repertory of traditional psalm-tunes in settings which had appeared in earlier British publications—a repertory of some seventy-five tunes, with many of the same tunes and settings passing from one collection to another. Their influence on Lyon's *Urania* is, however, rather difficult to establish exactly, because they were harmonized for two and three voices while Lyon's psalm tunes were set for four. Thus, when Lyon did take a tune from an American source, he added a fourth voice—the alto or "counter"—himself.[26] A comparison of *Urania* with earlier American collections leads to the conclusion that Lyon probably drew no more than six settings from them. But it would not be well to discount their influence on that basis. In all, twenty-four of the tunes in *Urania* had appeared in earlier American collections—roughly one-third of the American-published repertory to that date. While Lyon chose to print most in settings drawn from British collections, it may be that he first came to know some of these tunes through American printings.

This partial list of Lyon's sources shows that he became familiar with and drew upon a considerable range of music in putting *Urania* together. The collections upon which he relied most heavily (Arnold's *Compleat Psalmodist* and Ashworth's *Collection,* together with the American sources with which he was familiar) present mostly a standard repertory of already-accepted tunes. But the other collections represent a wide divergence. Adams's work is rich in mid-century tunes with changing textures; Smith's collection and Arnold's *Leicestershire Harmony* are devoted to newly-composed psalm-tunes in two slightly differing archaic styles; and many of the tunes in *Harmonia Sacra* are adaptations from Handel or Arne oratorios, or from modern popular songs.[27] A survey of *Urania*'s sources indicates that the range of James Lyon's musical taste was remarkably wide.

Although Lyon drew most of his tunes from earlier sources, he did not always print them exactly as he found them. Often his alterations took the form of embellishment, though generally not of the voice carrying the melody. CANTERBURY (p. 2) is an

example of Lyon's embellishmental technique at its simplest.[28] With the exception of the quarter-notes in the penultimate measure, all notes in the treble of less than half-note value were added by Lyon, apparently to give added melodic life to a voice which in its source, Arnold's *Compleat Psalmodist*, was relatively static. Similar touches occur in the treble of ST. DAVID'S (p. 8, phrase 2; the decoration in phrase 3 is original) and WESTMINSTER (p. 10, phrase 1), both also from Arnold, and in the bass of ANGELS HYMN (p. 36, phrase 3), taken from Ashworth's *Collection.*

Lyon added more extensive embellishments to other tunes. DORCHESTER (p. 23) is printed in a version very similar to that in Arnold, but the treble flourish in the chorus section (fifth full measure of that section) was Lyon's. And PSALM 136 (p. 80), also taken from Arnold, is supplied with a decorated version of the original treble, which had moved exclusively in whole-notes and half-notes. After composing a treble for the first phrase—Arnold's setting of the beginning is for three voices—Lyon went on to decorate Arnold's treble in phrases 2, 3, and 5; and he dissolved whole-notes in the treble's last two phrases into sixteenths.

Some of the tunes Lyon printed were originally set for three voices, and he filled them out with a fourth voice of his own. Six tunes in *Urania* have three voices which correspond convincingly with a three-voice American source, but their fourth voice, the "counter," which Lyon seems to have composed, violates orthodox eighteenth-century part-writing procedure. Generally, Lyon's counter harmonizes correctly with the other voices but lacks melodic independence. PSALM 119 OLD (p. 74) is a case in point, as five sets of parallel octaves appear between the counter and the other voices (phrases 1 and 2, tenor; phrases 5, 7, and 8, treble). While the other five tunes for which Lyon apparently composed the fourth voice (DERBY, PORTSMOUTH, PSALM 100 NEW, STANDISH, and ST. HUMPHREY) are less beset with parallels than OLD 119, all contain at least one set, betraying Lyon's hand. (The last [p. 14] also shows Lyon's propensity for ornamentation, this time especially in the bass.)

Lyon's responsibility for other settings may be suspected but is difficult to prove. For example, four tunes which had appeared in earlier American collections (MEAR, ISLE OF WIGHT, LONDON NEW, and BRUNSWICK) are printed in *Urania* in settings which do not correspond convincingly either with earlier American printings or with British settings the present author has examined. All display irregularities not characteristic of British practice. MEAR (p. 1) contains four sets of parallel octaves between counter and bass; ISLE OF WIGHT (p. 16), whose highly ornamented treble occasionally collides with the lower voices, comes to rest at the ends of its second and third phrases through remarkable harmonic progressions (so does the final phrase; but the difficulty is cleared up by reading the F in the penultimate measure of the counter as an engraving error for G); LONDON NEW (p. 17) again displays parallels between counter and bass (fifths in phrase 1; octaves in phrase 2), and a passage involving all four voices in the third phrase; and BRUNSWICK (p. 19), as well as one strange harmonic combination (phrase 2, beat 2), carries two sets of unequal fifths between counter and bass (phrases 1 and 4), and one set of parallel octaves between counter and treble (phrase 4). Perhaps Lyon came upon settings

similar to these in a source yet undiscovered, but it is more likely that he began with the known American versions and made his own changes—a supposition supported by the fact that ISLE OF WIGHT, LONDON NEW, and BRUNSWICK are printed on consecutive pages together with PORTSMOUTH, a tune whose setting Lyon certainly took from an American source.

The most problematical composition in *Urania* remains to be discussed. Sonneck had words of praise for Henry Dawkins, the engraver of *Urania*, though he did point out that the work is plagued with "numerous errors" (p. 160). PSALM 119 NEW (p. 76) was Dawkins's worst botch. In the second half of the piece (p. 77) he somehow managed to reverse the order of the two eight-bar phrases in the tenor and bass parts so that phrase 4 of the original tenor and bass accompanies phrase 3 of the treble and counter, while phrase 3 of the tenor and bass is set with the final phrase of the upper two voices. (Cf. Plate III.) The result is as sour a little piece as one could imagine. As changes in the engraving on p. 77 show, Dawkins's mistake did not go entirely unnoticed. Someone, probably Lyon himself, for he must have examined the proofs, discovered something amiss and recommended corrections in an attempt to expunge at least some of the dissonance which had crept in. Accordingly, the first treble note on p. 77, a *G* in the original, was changed to *F♯* and the last counter note of the same phrase, an *F♯*, was changed to *E*. In the final phrase, the tenor's beginning *B-E-D♯-E* was changed to *B-C-D-E*, and treble and counter were altered in measures 5 and 6 of that phrase: treble from *A-B-E-D* to the present *B-B-D-D*, and counter from *F♯-D-E-G* to *E-D-D-G*. These alterations succeed in removing some of the more jarring vertical errors from the

PSALM CXIX.

Blef--fed are they that per-fect are, and pure in mind and heart:

Blef--fed are they that give themfelves, his fta-tutes to ob-ferve:

Whofe lives and con-- ver-fa--tions do, from God's laws ne--ver ftart.

Seek--ing the Lord with all their hearts, and ne--ver from him fwerve.

Plate III. Psalm 119 from Davenport, *Psalm-Singer's Pocket Companion*, 2nd edition, London, 1758, p. 43.
Courtesy of The Library of Congress.

piece, but they have no effect whatever on the passage's progression of harmony, which remains, in a word, a mess.

Lyon's difficulty with PSALM 119 NEW helps to define the limits of his musicianship. Putting it simply, Lyon possessed certain innate musical gifts, and he managed in the course of his musical experience to pick up some basic rules about consonance and dissonance and a rather shaky command of part-writing. But what stood beyond his knowledge was the system of functional harmony—of established chord connections—rooted in the principles of thoroughbass, which lay implicit in the theory and practice of most British psalmodists. And that should not be surprising, for the works from which Lyon probably received much of his theoretical know-how, Arnold's *Compleat Psalmodist* and Tans'ur's *Royal Melody Compleat*, did not touch on that subject at all, confining their instructions to a classification of concords and discords, and to part-writing advice.

As noted above, all extant copies of *Urania* are identical in musical content. Had James Lyon used *Urania* in singing-schools and retained a proprietary interest in it after its initial publication, it is reasonable to assume that he would have noticed at least its more obvious errors and seen to it that they were corrected in later printings. There is no evidence to indicate that he did. Thus, NEW 119, taken together with what is known about Lyon's life, helps to support the conclusion that though he remained active as a composer into the mid-1770's and perhaps later, his professional interest in music began to decline after *Urania* was published.

*   *   *   *

THE DESCENDENTS OF *URANIA*

Within three years of its publication *Urania* was circulating in Boston. Josiah Flagg's *Collection of the Best Psalm Tunes* (Boston, 1764; mentioned above) carried MORNING HYMN, attributed to Lyon, and when the same compiler's *Sixteen Anthems* appeared two years later, it was advertised in the *Massachusetts Gazette and Boston News-Letter* of October 2, 1766, as containing, together with the anthems, "some tunes from Lion, Smith, Ravencraft, &c."[29] Flagg surely took DAGENHAM, one of the tunes in his anthem collection, from *Urania*.

Daniel Bayley (c. 1725–1799) of Newburyport, Massachusetts, was America's most prolific compiler of tunebooks during the period before the Revolution, and in 1769 he capitalized on a shortcut offered by the difficulty of enforcing copyright restrictions between Great Britain and her colonies. One recalls the selectivity which James Lyon had exercised in choosing the music for *Urania*; Bayley's method of selection was quite different. He brought out under a single cover, re-engraved, two British tunebooks which in their original form had become popular in the colonies: Tans'ur's *Royal Melody Compleat* (London, 1755), and Aaron Williams's *Universal Psalmodist* (London, 1763). Bayley's reprint, which with a certain gall he named *American Harmony*, was not an exact duplicate of the original works, and for his minor additions to Tans'ur and Williams he turned, among others, to Lyon's *Urania*. The anthem, "Let the shrill trumpet's," usually attributed to Lyon himself and heretofore published only in *Urania*, appears in the *American Harmony*. Surely Lyon's music received greater New

England circulation through Bayley's collection than through his own, for the *American Harmony* was reissued five times between 1769 and 1774.

Lyon's influence can also be seen in two other collections Bayley published in the 1770's. The *New Universal Harmony* (Newburyport, 1773) includes the first American printing since *Urania* of PSALM 15; it also includes MARRIAGE HYMN by Lyon, the first of several compositions which had not appeared in *Urania* but which Lyon contributed to other compilers' collections. The next year Bayley published John Stickney's *Gentleman and Lady's Companion*, much of it printed from the same plates as the *American Harmony*. Stickney's work shared a number of tunes with *Urania*, including Hopkinson's PSALM 23 (in a four-voice setting which only a misprint in the bass prevents from being identical with Lyon's). Furthermore, Stickney's collection included two new compositions, FRIENDSHIP and MACHIAS, which, though unattributed in the *Companion*, have been identified as Lyon's own.[30] The appearance in Bayley's and Stickney's collections of previously unpublished music by Lyon provides evidence both of Lyon's continued activity as a composer and his continued contact with New England compilers. It is not unlikely that the two compilers received Lyon's works from the composer himself, perhaps during the year 1773, when he is known to have spent time away from Machias.

Andrew Law (1749–1821) of Connecticut seems to have admired *Urania* more than any other New England compiler. His appropriation of the design of *Urania*'s title-page for his *Select Harmony* (Cheshire, 1779) has already been noted. But his approval of the music in *Urania* was equally strong. Between 1779 and 1783 Law brought out three other publications: the *Select Number of Plain Tunes* ([Cheshire, 1781]), the *Collection of Hymn Tunes* (Cheshire, [1783]), and the *Rudiments of Music* ([Cheshire], 1783). All four collections include compositions previously available in America only in *Urania*, in settings which correspond convincingly with Lyon's. By the mid-1790's Law had begun to print most tunes with the melody in the treble rather than the tenor, rearranging settings himself and making it impossible to trace with any certainty the source from which he obtained a tune. But the peripatetic Law was still carrying Lyon's collection around in his trunk as late as 1797,[31] and it seems no coincidence that his shape-note *Musical Primer* (Cambridge, 1803) contains fifteen tunes which had appeared in *Urania*.

Simeon Jocelin (1746–1823) was another Connecticut compiler who knew *Urania*; and a comparison between the first and second editions of his *Chorister's Companion* (New Haven, 1782 and 1788) suggests that he knew James Lyon as well. The earlier *Companion* carried several tunes which had not appeared in America since Lyon's collection, and their settings are virtually identical with Lyon's. But during the half-dozen years separating the first and second editions, Jocelin received new information about the composers of some of the tunes his work shares with *Urania*, for he changed one attribution and added several more. He also added music to his new edition, including a brand new setting of PSALM 17 by James Lyon. The appearance of PSALM 17 and the new attributions indicate, if they do not prove, that Jocelin was in contact with Lyon himself at some time between 1782 and 1788.[32] And that period coincides with one of Lyon's absences from Machias, the years 1783–1785.

At least two New England tunebooks of the 1790's demonstrate that *Urania* was still being used as a source. Daniel Read's *Columbian Harmonist* No. 2 (New Haven, [1794]) includes nine tunes which had appeared in *Urania*. Of the nine, eight had also been reprinted many times throughout the 1770's and 1780's; but GLOUCESTER, which Read presented in a version identical to Lyon's, had not appeared in any American collection since *Urania*. Finally, Jonathan Benjamin's *Harmonia Coelestis* (Northampton, 1799) contains four compositions—three of the four printed on successive pages—which the compiler surely found in *Urania*, in similar settings. And if more evidence is needed to establish a link between the two works, the titles provide it. *Urania* and *Harmonia Coelestis*, with Samuel Holyoke's *Harmonia Americana* (Boston, 1791), are the only American tunebooks of the eighteenth century to carry non-English titles.

The traceable influence of *Urania* on New England tunebooks was remarkable; but, as one might expect from its place of issue, its effect on Philadelphia tunebooks was even more telling. Some eighty-five different eighteenth-century American publications of sacred music are extant; only ten were published in Philadelphia. But of the ten, only the latest, *New Jersey Harmony* (1797) appears not to have been influenced by *Urania*.

Within two years of *Urania*'s appearance two other collections of tunes were published in Philadelphia. The compilers of neither were announced on their title-pages, but one, *Tunes in Three Parts* (1763) was published by Anthony Armbruster, and Sonneck has shown that the other, *A Collection of Psalm Tunes* (1763), was compiled by Francis Hopkinson. The former, besides duplicating much of *Urania*'s repertory, includes a tune, WATTS's PSALM 104, which had been first published in that collection, which the compiler called LYON. As for the latter, Francis Hopkinson and James Lyon must have known each other. Both appeared as composers at the commencement exercises of the College of Philadelphia (University of Pennsylvania) in May, 1761, and Lyon printed Hopkinson's setting of Psalm 23 in *Urania*. Hopkinson's *Collection* shares nearly two-thirds of its repertory with *Urania*, including Lyon's setting of WATTS's PSALM 104, thus demonstrating that Hopkinson was familiar with the earlier work.

The appearance in Philadelphia of three different tunebooks in two years' time represents, as it turns out, only a deceptive flurry; not until the 1780's was another sacred collection published there. Two works from that decade display familiarity with *Urania*, but only slight evidence of its influence. The brief and anonymous *Tunes Suited to the Psalms and Hymns of the Book of Common Prayer* was designed to be bound in at the end of a version of the *Book of Common Prayer* (Philadelphia, 1786) adapted specifically for Americans; this collection carries Lyon's setting of WATTS's PSALM 104. So, surprisingly, does the century's only American publication of music for Roman Catholic worship, John Aitken's *Compilation of the Litanies and Vespers* (1787). Aitken's work also includes a musically identical version of *Urania*'s SALISBURY.

If James Lyon was Philadelphia's most outstanding

psalmodist before the War of Independence, Andrew Adgate (1762–1793) was the leader after. Determining the precise extent of Lyon's influence on Adgate introduces another topic for consideration: the origin and influence of Lyon's title, *Urania*. For it is a fact that during his brief career as a public musician Adgate lost no opportunity to identify himself with the label "Uranian," and under that title he carried on most of his organized musical activity.[33]

It is not known whether Adgate and Lyon ever met. But Adgate admired Lyon enough as a composer to include his anthem, "The Lord Descended from Above," in his well-known concert of sacred music in April, 1786, and Lyon's FRIENDSHIP appeared on the program of the first "Uranian Concert" a year later.[34] In addition, Adgate borrowed some music from *Urania*, as described below. The musical and geographical links which existed between the two men makes one suspect that Adgate arrived at his Uranian motif with Lyon in mind. And his choice hints that he believed at least some Philadelphians would associate "Uranian" with sacred music, suggesting that Lyon's collection still carried some reputation in the 1780's.

A careful, if not exhaustive search through musical and mythological sources has turned up no special identification of the muse Urania with music. And neither of the two earlier musical works the present author has discovered with "Urania" in their titles could have had any influence on James Lyon.[35] In the absence of evidence to the contrary, it can be supposed that Lyon thought of the title himself, and that he was therefore responsible for the rubric which graced much of Philadelphia's late eighteenth-century musical life.[36]

As noted, the music of *Urania* exerted some influence on Adgate's *Philadelphia Harmony* (1789). Adgate's work contains fifteen tunes from Lyon's collection, eleven in settings very close or identical to the settings in *Urania*. It is true that Adgate's collection presents a repertory very similar to Andrew Law's collections, and that he could have taken some from Law rather than Lyon, but of the ten compositions in the *Philadelphia Harmony* that Adgate could not have taken from Law, eight were American tunes of the 1770's and 1780's, and the other two, BRUNSWICK and ST. HUMPHREY'S, had appeared in *Urania* in versions bearing similarities to Adgate's. Further evidence that Adgate was influenced by *Urania* is found in Part II of the *Philadelphia Harmony*, first issued separately in 1791 and then appearing as part of all later editions. Part II carries twenty-nine compositions, seven of which had appeared in *Urania*, including Lyon's setting of WATTS'S PSALM 104.[37]

In 1788 there appeared in Philadelphia a collection which more than any other demonstrates *Urania*'s influence: the anonymous *Selection of Sacred Harmony*. Of the *Selection*'s sixty-two tunes, thirty-two had appeared in *Urania*, all but two in settings which correspond convincingly with Lyon's. Furthermore, nine of those either appeared in an American publication for the first time since *Urania*, or they appeared *in that setting* for the first time since *Urania*. It is only fair to mention, though, that later editions of the *Selection* (five editions of the work were issued in all, the last in 1797) omitted some of the less popular tunes from Lyon's collection, so that in its final form it carries only twenty.

Two Philadelphia publications of the 1790's complete the list of eighteenth-century collections which show some evidence of having been influenced by *Urania*, though perhaps not directly. Nehemiah Shumway's compendious *American Harmony* (1793) shares eleven tunes with Lyon's collection—seven in settings which correspond convincingly with Lyon's. But the seven were part of a central repertory which appeared in many collections and cannot be unmistakably traced to Lyon's. Finally, John Poor's *Collection of Psalms and Hymns* (1794), a small book appearing in only one edition, includes the Philadelphia favorite, Lyon's setting of WATTS's PSALM 104.

*   *   *   *

Some details remain to be uncovered before the full story of *Urania* is told, but the work's significance can still be assessed. *Urania* did not appear in a vacuum; it was the first important American contribution to a tradition of British psalmody already well established in the Colonies. Though drawn mostly from British sources, *Urania* was an American product, or to be more accurate, it was the product of a single American, James Lyon, who wrote the introduction, chose the music, reworked many of the settings, and even provided a few tunes of his own. Lyon succeeded in making *Urania* one of the most comprehensive collections of music published in America during the eighteenth century, generously covering all the forms and styles of contemporaneous psalmody. As a musician Lyon never attained a sure grasp of the idiom of European composers. Yet, curiously enough, when American musical reformers began in the 1790's to clamor against the crudeness of their countrymen's music and to devote their own collections mostly to European

tunes, Lyon was not one of the targets for their scorn. Even reformers like Andrew Law and Jonathan Benjamin were still using *Urania* as a source some four decades after its first publication.

Richard Crawford

Ann Arbor, Michigan
May 1970

FOOTNOTES FOR PREFACE

[1] *Pennsylvania Journal* (Philadelphia, May 22, 1760). Quoted in Oscar G. T. Sonneck, *Francis Hopkinson and James Lyon* (Washington: McQueen, 1905; reprinted, New York: Da Capo Press, 1967), 135. Sonneck's twin monograph, though more than sixty years old, is factually reliable and more detailed in certain matters than this Preface. The Preface, in fact, should be considered as an emendation of Sonneck's essay on Lyon's *Urania*, and readers familiar with Sonneck's work will notice that it has been organized under his chapter headings. The scholar will find Sonneck's work a necessary companion piece to this volume.

[2] Sonneck, *Hopkinson and Lyon*, 121–33, contains most of the information presented here, and page references in the following paragraphs pertain also to that work. An article on Lyon by Frederick W. Coburn, *Dictionary of American Biography*, Allen Johnson & Dumas Malone, eds. (New York: Scribner's, 1928–44), XI, 530, supplies additional data.

[3] The quotation is taken from the diary of Philip Vickers Fithian (1747–1776) of the Princeton Class of 1772. Quoted in Sonneck, 186.

[4] See William Otis Sawtelle, "Acadia: the Pre-Loyalist Migration and the Philadelphia Plantation," *Pennsylvania Magazine* (Philadelphia: Pennsylvania Historical Society, 1927), LI, 244–85.

[5] Ibid., 277*n.*

[6] James Phinney Baxter, ed. *Documentary History of the State of Maine*

(Portland: Lefavor-Tower, 1910), XV, 8; in *Collections and Proceedings of the Maine Historical Society*, 2nd Series.

[7] Peter Force, ed., *American Archives* (Washington, 1843), 4th Series, IV, 460–61.

[8] Baxter, ed., *Documentary History*, XIV, 173.

[9] Rev. Charles H. Pope, "Machias in the Revolution," in *Collections and Proceedings of the Maine Historical Society* (Portland: The Society, 1895), 2nd Series, VI, 129–31.

[10] Force, ed., *American Archives* (Washington, 1848), 5th Series, I, 1280–83.

[11] Baxter, ed., *Documentary History*, XV, 7. I have made some minor changes in the original punctuation.

[12] Near the end of his life Lyon worked on a series of scriptural meditations, which he called *The Saint's Daily Assistant*. According to the title-page, one meditation for each day of the year was planned. A group of thirty-one appeared in 1791, and another group of twenty-nine was published in 1793, the two collections apparently covering January and February. Lyon died before more of the work could be printed. See Charles Evans, *American Bibliography* (Chicago: Blakely; Worcester: American Antiquarian Society, 1903–59), No. 23516 and No. 25737.

[13] The grandson of one of America's pioneer printers, the elder William Bradford, and a nephew of Andrew Bradford, founder of the earliest newspaper in the Middle Colonies, William Bradford was born to his trade. He founded a newspaper of his own, the *Pennsylvania Journal*, which continued for more than half a century (1742–1793); operated a coffeehouse frequented by Philadelphia's men of trade; and served during the Revolutionary War as printer to the Continental Congress. See *Dictionary of American Biography*, II, 564–66. Evans, *American Bibliography*, lists the first edition of *Urania* as No. 8906 and identifies Bradford as the printer.

[14] Dawkins was born in England, emigrated to New York around 1753, and by 1757 had settled in Philadelphia. His later years were marred by arrests for counterfeiting, and he disappears from view after 1780. See *Dictionary of American Biography*, V, 150–51.

[15] Common meter refers to a four-line text whose lines are alternately composed of eight and six syllables (8. 6. 8. 6.). A long-meter text encompasses four eight-syllable lines. Short meter is arranged as follows: (6. 6. 8. 6.). In the first group of psalm-tunes, COOKFIELD (p. 20) is out of place. Set in long meter, it is preceded by nineteen common-meter tunes and followed by four more. WIRKSWORTH (p. 25) is the first of six short-meter tunes, and BATH (p. 31) is the first of six tunes in long meter. Two relatively elaborate common-meter tunes, LEATHERED and CRANLEY (p. 37–39), round out the first section.

[16] Some American compilers made a distinction between "anthem" and "set-piece." The latter resembled the anthem in size and style, containing word repetitions and textural changes, but its text was metrical poetry while anthem texts were prose. A set-piece provides a through-composed setting of two or more stanzas of rhymed text, unlike the strophic psalm-tune, which provides only one. Three of Lyon's "anthems" qualify as "set-pieces," according to this definition: "The Lord Descended" (p. 125), "Jehovah Reigns" (p. 133), and "Let the Shrill Trumpet's" (p. 165).

For a more detailed description of the kind of anthem Lyon published see Ralph T. Daniel, *The Anthem in New England before 1800* (Evanston: Northwestern University Press, 1966), 47–52. See also W. Thomas Marrocco, "The Set Piece," *Journal of the American Musicological Society*, XV/3 (Fall 1962), 348–52.

[17] The fuging-tune was developed by mid-eighteenth-century British psalmodists and was cultivated by American composers late in that century. While variations in the form occur, it most typically is divided into two sections as follows: the beginning is brief and in block-chord texture; the second section begins with a point of imitation (the "fuge"), and then returns for its conclusion to the chordal texture of the beginning. The second section is usually repeated. Since the fuging-tune bears no formal relation to the classical fugue, it seems sensible to follow the suggestion put forth by Irving Lowens, that the distinction between the two forms be emphasized by adopting the spelling "fuging-tune" used by most eighteenth-century compilers. See Irving Lowens, "The Origins of the American Fuging-Tune," *Journal of the American Musicological Society*, V/1 (Spring 1953); revised in Lowens, *Music and Musicians in Early America* (New York: Norton, 1964), 237–48.

[18] The six compositions Lyon designated as "new"—four psalm and hymn-tunes, and two anthems—will require a little more examination, since they remain among the very earliest identified American compositions. Sonneck believed that Lyon himself composed all six, and his opinion has been generally

accepted by later scholars. But it now appears that although there is no reason to dispute Lyon's authorship of four of the six, he probably did not compose the fifth and surely not the sixth.

It is safe to assume that WATTS'S PSALM 104 and "The Lord Descended from Above" were composed by Lyon. Two years after *Urania* appeared in print, a collection of tunes was published by Anthony Armbruster in Philadelphia, containing the setting of WATTS'S PSALM 104; the tune was entitled LYON. Later Philadelphia printings of the tune were also attributed to Lyon, though it bore his name as title only in Armbruster's printing. (Lyon may have composed two more of the "new" tunes, PSALM 8 and PSALM 95, but later attributions are no help here, since neither was reprinted after *Urania*.) As for "The Lord Descended from Above," it is attributed to Lyon in the program of one of Andrew Adgate's Philadelphia concerts in 1786. (See O.G.T. Sonneck, *Early Concert-Life in America* [Leipzig: Breitkopf & Härtel, 1907; reprinted, New York: Musurgia, 1949], 108.) But the same program includes another of *Urania's* "new" compositions, "Let the shrill Trumpet's," without attribution. That Adgate, who presumably would have known, assigned "The Lord Descended from Above" to Lyon and did not name the composer of "Let the shrill Trumpet's," the work which precedes it on the program, makes it seem unlikely that Lyon wrote the latter, especially since all but two of the ten compositions on the concert are provided with attributions. It is certain that the final "new" tune, PSALM 23, was not Lyon's. Robert Stevenson has identified Francis Hopkinson as its composer. (See Appendix II, Index of Compositions.)

[19] Francis Hopkinson (1737–1791), jurist, author, and signer of the Declaration of Independence, became the first native-born American to publish a collection of secular music when his *Seven Songs* for voice and harpsichord appeared in Philadelphia (1788). Unquestionably Philadelphia's leading musical amateur, Hopkinson was active from the 1750's until his death. While he seems to have been interested chiefly in chamber music and song, he also composed some psalm-tunes, and he brought out the *Collection* cited here, as well as a metrical psalter for the Dutch Reformed Church of New York City. See Sonneck, *Hopkinson and Lyon*, for the most detailed treatment available.

[20] See note 25.

[21] It might also be worth noting that some of the subscribers continued to support music in later years. An advertisement for Andrew Adgate's Uranian Academy in 1787 lists a half-dozen among the patrons: John Bayard, John Ewing, Charles Pettit, Benjamin Rush, Isaac Snowden, and William Young. See Sonneck, *Early Concert-Life*, 106.

[22] Clarence S. Brigham, *Paul Revere's Engravings* (Worcester: American Antiquarian Society, 1954; reprinted, New York: Atheneum, 1969), 16–18. Irving Lowens, "Andrew Law and the Pirates," *Journal of the American Musicological Society*, XIII (1960), 208 & plate 1; revised in Lowens, *Music and Musicians*, 62–63.

[23] *Harmonia Sacra* carries no date, but most references place it around 1760. However, since Lyon drew music from it, and since it is clear that he had finished compiling *Urania* by May of that year, it is unlikely that *Harmonia Sacra* was issued as late as 1760. For more on the date of *Harmonia Sacra*, see Maurice Frost, ed., *Historical Companion to Hymns Ancient & Modern* (London: Clowes, 1962), 99n.

[24] Henry Dawkins does not get high marks from those who have compared his work with other American engravers of the time. David M. Stauffer, *American Engravers upon Copper and Steel*, Part I (New York: Grolier Club, 1907), evaluates his book-plates, bill-heads, and map ornamentation as "fairly good" (p. 61), but says of his only portrait plate that it was "atrociously drawn and poorly engraved" (p. 62). Joseph Jackson's article on Dawkins in the *Dictionary of American Biography* states that "[he] was notorious for his poor equipment for the higher forms of engraving which he essayed" (p. 151), but offers no criteria for that judgement. Dawkins is treated at somewhat greater length in Charles Dexter Allen's *American Book-Plates* (New York & London: Macmillan, 1894), where he is identified as a purveyor of "debased Chippendale" style (p. 53), because he had a tendency to include in some bookplates what the author considers incongruous mixtures of objects and excessive detail. Allen, however, does admit that some of Dawkins's less elaborate book-plates are acceptable examples of Chippendale (p. 128); it would seem that the title page of *Urania* should be included among them. Having examined twenty-odd surviving book-plates Dawkins is known to have engraved, Allen observes that the engraver's designs "are variations of one general plan, which seems to have been borrowed from an English-made plate," and calls Dawkins "an engraver of but few original ideas . . . largely a copyist" (p. 127). Allen's conclusion supports the contention offered here: that Dawkins's idea for the title page of *Urania* was not

original. But in fairness to Dawkins it should be reiterated that his work is outstanding when compared with that of other eighteenth-century American music engravers. And it should also be noted that originality had not yet become the *sine qua non* it is today, so that copying another's work was a generally accepted practice among eighteenth-century engravers. (Much of Brigham, *Paul Revere's Engravings* is devoted to demonstrating that fact. See especially Brigham's comment on p. 56.)

The following hypothesis about the title page of *Urania* seems plausible: James Lyon admired the title page of *Harmonia Sacra*, and when he hired Dawkins to engrave *Urania* he suggested *Harmonia Sacra* as a model. Dawkins retained some of its features, though he omitted the angels—he was not, we remember from Stauffer, a good drawer—and he based his border on the trusty Chippendale style which he had mastered in making book-plates, modifying its shape to conform to the tunebook format.

[25] Sonneck identifies the fourth edition of Arnold's *Compleat Psalmodist* (London, 1756) and William Tans'ur's *Royal Melody Compleat* (London, 1756) as Lyon's sources (p. 166–68).

[26] Virtually all eighteenth-century American collections assign the melody of their psalm-tunes to the tenor. In three-voice settings, bass and soprano ("treble") are added; in four-voice settings, treble, tenor, and bass are joined by an alto, or "counter."

[27] Frost, *Historical Companion*, 99.

[28] I have examined numerous settings of the tunes discussed in this paragraph and the next, and have found that Lyon's settings are almost identical with those to which they are compared. Since it has been established that Lyon drew music from both Arnold's and Ashworth's collections, the assumption is made that he found the settings there and added his own embellishments. While the possibility remains that Lyon found the settings he printed in sources not yet located, and that the embellishments were not his at all, it seems more likely that my assumption is correct.

[29] Quoted in Brigham, *Paul Revere's Engravings*, 38. See also Sonneck, *Hopkinson and Lyon*, 181.

[30] Sonneck (*Hopkinson and Lyon*, 189–93) shows that FRIENDSHIP was composed by Lyon. As for MACHIAS, it appeared under the title PSALM 19 in Andrew Law's *Rudiments of Music* (3rd edition, 1791; 4th edition, 1792). In the later printing Law named Lyon as the composer.

[31] See Richard A. Crawford, *Andrew Law, American Psalmodist* (Evanston: Northwestern University Press, 1968), 136.

[32] In the second edition of the *Chorister's Companion* Jocelin attributed four tunes to William Tuckey, an English-born musician who emigrated to America about 1753; three of the four had also appeared in the first edition of Jocelin's work, two without attribution (PSALM 9 and PSALM 33, both from *Urania*), and one (PSALM 24) ascribed to a composer named Brown, who was identified as an American. Clearly, between 1782 and 1788 Jocelin was given reason to believe that Tuckey had composed the three tunes. The fourth composition attributed to Tuckey, PSALM 67, complicates the question, for Jocelin's was its first American printing. Where did Jocelin get it? Surely not from Tuckey himself, for he had died seven years earlier. If it could be proved that Jocelin had some personal contact with Lyon, it would be logical to assume that he received the information which caused him to change his attributions—and perhaps even received Tuckey's setting of PSALM 67—from Lyon himself. The appearance of Lyon's own new setting of PSALM 17 in *The Chorister's Companion* of 1788 would seem to provide that proof.

[33] Adgate's musical career has been traced no earlier than 1783, when he served as an assistant at a Philadelphia singing-school conducted by Andrew Law, also an admirer of *Urania*. (See Crawford, *Andrew Law*, 63–69, for an account of the acrimonious relationship between Law and Adgate.) On the first day of 1785 a pamphlet appeared in Philadelphia, *Introductory Lessons, Practiced by the Uranian Society*. The pamphlet seems to have been Adgate's, and the "Uranian Society" was his singing-school. (For the attribution see Allen P. Britton, "Theoretical Introductions in American Tunebooks to 1800" [unpublished Ph.D. dissertation, Department of Music, University of Michigan, 1949], 580.) By the next year Adgate's Society had become the Uranian Academy, a series of concerts he presented in 1787 were called Uranian Concerts, and Adgate adorned himself with the title P.U.A.—President of the Uranian Academy—on the title pages of his two major publications: *Rudiments of Music* (Philadelphia, 1788), and *Philadelphia Harmony* (1789). For more on Adgate, see Sonneck, *Early Concert-Life*, 103–20.

[34] Sonneck, *Early Concert-Life*, 108, 114.

[35] Michael Praetorius, *Urania oder Urano-Chorodia* (Wolffenbüttel, [1613]) is a collection of German polychoral sacred compositions; Antonio del Riccio, *Urania Armonica* (Florence, 1686) is a solo cantata. It is most unlikely that James Lyon would have known of either.

[36] In Greek mythology, the nine Muses had the ability to inspire anyone to write poetry or to tell stories. By extension, they came to be patronesses of all the arts. The identification of specific Muses with specific arts, according to H. J. Rose, was not a part of the original story, and the identifications vary from author to author. Rose dismisses such identifications as "silliness . . . which a very small knowledge of classical literature is sufficient to refute." See Rose, *Handbook of Greek Mythology*, 5th edition (New York: Dutton, n.d.), 174*n*. Nevertheless, the associations were made during the Christian era, and the picture on Lyon's title page leaves no doubt that the Urania who appears there is the muse of astronomy.

One can advance two reasons Lyon might have chosen to name his collection after Urania: her association with the heavens, and the euphony and comparative pronounceability of her name. Prefaces to many eighteenth-century American tunebooks deal with the matter of pronunciation, and when one reads of the errors which were common, he applauds Lyon's judgment for not naming his collection after some of Urania's sister Muses—Polyhymnia, for example, or Calliope, or Euterpe.

[37] Adgate printed most of the tunes he seems to have taken from *Urania* in two-voice settings. But those two voices are virtually identical to the corresponding voices in Lyon's settings. This fact along with the other circumstances linking the two men make it likely that *Urania* was Adgate's source.

APPENDIX I: EDITIONS OF *URANIA*

One of the most valuable portions of Sonneck's work on *Urania* was his observation of differences between copies. As noted above, he distinguished five editions or printings, and the findings he presents in *Francis Hopkinson and James Lyon*, pages 137–47, combined with a few details I have added, are rearranged below to provide a quick means of identifying the various printings. Three points of difference are noted: 1) Collation; 2) Location of asterisks; 3) Differences in typeset material.

1. *Collation*. Setting aside the matter of missing pages, two forms can easily be distinguished. Collation A is assumed to represent the first edition, Collation B to represent all others.

A	B
1 p. l., 2 p., 3 l., xii, 198 p.	1 p. l., 2 p., 1 l., xii, 198 p.
Title-page, *recto* p. l. *Verso* blank.	Title-page, *recto* p. l. *Verso* blank.
Dedication, p. [1]–2.	Dedication, p. [1]–2.
"Index," *recto* 1st l. *Verso* blank.	"Index," *recto* l. *Verso* blank.
"Subscribers Names," *recto* & *verso* 2nd l., *recto* 3rd l. *Verso* blank.	
Instructions, p. I–XII.	Instructions, p. I–XII.
Music, p. 1–198.	Music, p. 1–198.

2. *Location of asterisks*. Later editions display asterisks identifying the compositions on pages 44, 50, 63, 125, 165, and 194 as "new." The first edition exists in two forms: one lacks asterisks on pages 50 and 165 but carries the remaining four; the other contains five, lacking only the one on page 50.[1]

3. *Differences in typeset material*. On page [1] the word "America" in the third line of the dedication is printed in two different ways, as indicated. The tops of the last three columns (columns 3, 4, and 5) of the index show variations in the way Psalm 102 is identified, in the spelling of STANDISH, and in the printing of the anthem title, "Is there not an ap-

pointed time." The reader will also note that in one printing (IV) the third and fourth columns begin with different titles than the corresponding columns of the other five.

Table I conveys these differences in typeset material and shows where copies are presently located. State I is the first edition,[2] States II and III[3] are those which Sonneck assigned conjecturally to Philadelphia (1767) and New York (1773), States IV and V are variants for which he suggested no date, and State VI is a variant Sonneck did not discover.[4] Copies listed as "unidentified" lack the pages which would make identification possible.

FOOTNOTES FOR APPENDIX I

[1] The copy owned by The Library of Congress is the only one found to have five asterisks. Sonneck suggests (p. 145) that the omission of the asterisk on page 165 was probably discovered while the first edition was still in the press. It seems likely that the omission on page 50 was not noticed until the first printing had been completed.

[2] The Library of Congress copy is reproduced as No. 8908 in the Readex Microprint edition of Charles Evans's *American Bibliography* and thus may be examined in any library owning the microprint of Evans.

[3] The New York Historical Society copy is reproduced as No. 12839 in the Readex Microprint edition of Evans.

[4] In making his bibliographical study of *Urania* Sonneck examined thirteen copies, and in the present listing of extant copies Sonneck's designations appear in parentheses. Of the thirteen copies Sonneck looked at, nine may still be found in the libraries in which he saw them, two (Y.U. II and Pa. H.S. II) seem no longer to be there, and the two privately owned copies Sonneck examined have not been traced. However, nearly a dozen additional copies have turned up, and I have obtained some information about all but two of them. (The two are mentioned by Robert Stevenson in *Protestant Church Music in America*, 51–52. One is located on Antigua of the Leeward Islands, perhaps having been carried there by one of Lyon's subscribers, "Master Hunt of Antigua." The other may be found among the Telfair Family Papers in the Georgia Historical Society.)

I wish to thank Miss Mary Brown of the American Antiquarian Society, Mrs. Ruth Bleeker of the Boston Public Library, Mr. Theodore Finney of the Pittsburgh Theological Seminary, Mr. James Irvine of the Princeton Theological Seminary, and Mr. Karl Kroeger of Providence, Rhode Island, for supplying information about copies of *Urania*.

TABLE I

	I	II	III	IV	V	VI	VII
p. [1], line 3: Index, col. 3:	*America* ————102 112	AMERICA New 102 ————112	*America* Psalm 102 112	*America* New 113 Old 119	[page missing] New 102 ========112	[page missing] ————102 112	*Unidentified copies*
col. 4:	Southwell Standwich	Southwell Standwich	Southwell Standish	Westminster Willington	Southwell Standwich	Southwell Standish	

col. 5:	O praise the Lord
	Is there not
	  an appoint.
	  ed Time
		O praise the Lord
		Is there not an ap-
		  pointed Time,
			O praise the Lord
			Is there not
			  an appoint-
			  ed Time
				HYMNS.
				St. Matthew's
				Palmy's
					[page mutilated]	O praise the Lord
						Is there not an
						  appointed
						  Time	

Copies:[4]	Baylor U. (repro- duced here), Brown U.'s John Carter Brown Library, Library of Con- gress (L.C.), New York Public Library (N.Y.P.L.), Pennsylvania Historical So- ciety (Pa. H.S. I)	Brown U.'s John Hay Library, Pittsburgh The- ological Semi- nary (Warr. I), Yale U.'s Beinecke Li- brary (Y.U. I)	New York His- torical Society (N.Y.H.S.)	Boston Public Library, Mass- achusetts His- torical Society (M.H.S. I), U. of Michigan's Clements Library	Yale U. (Y.U. II)	Princeton Theo- logical Seminary	American Anti- quarian Society, Massachusetts Historical Society (Mass. H.S. II), Pennsylvania Historical Society (Pa. H.S. II), Pittsburgh Theo- logical Seminary (Warr. II), Princeton Theo- logical Seminary, Trinity College's Watkinson Library

APPENDIX II: INDEX OF COMPOSITIONS

The index of compositions lists psalm-tunes and hymn-tunes together and treats anthems as a separate category. Tune titles appear as in *Urania*'s index. Composer attributions are all editorial, since Lyon included none himself.

The second column of the index identifies first printings of tunes. Secondary sources which supply documentation are indicated by the following code:

Frost *E&S*   Frost, Maurice. *English & Scottish Psalm & Hymn Tunes c. 1543–1677*. London: Oxford University Press, 1953. (Frost's tune numbers are included because his work lacks a title index.)

Frost *HC*   ——— (ed.). *Historical Companion to Hymns Ancient & Modern*. London: William Clowes, .1962.

Hymns A&M   *Hymns Ancient and Modern*. Historical edition. London: William Clowes, 1909.

Lightwood   Lightwood, James. *The Music of the Methodist Hymn-book*. London: Epworth Press, 1935.

Lowens   Lowens, Irving. "The First American Music Textbook," *Music and Musicians in Early America*. New York: W. W. Norton, 1964.

First printings not documented in the index are: tunes Lyon claimed as first printings, which are designated "1st pr. (Lyon)"; tunes attributed to European composers who emigrated to the Colonies, which are designated "1st pr."; and tunes identified as first printings by the compilers of collections in which they appeared (the tunes traced to Arnold's *Leicestershire Harmony*, Smith's *Set*, and Knapp's *Sett*).

The third column of the index shows the collection from which it seems likely that Lyon took his setting of a given tune. If the setting is printed under a title other than its title in *Urania*, the second title is supplied in a footnote. Usually only one source is listed for each tune; more appear only where it has proved impossible to determine which one served as Lyon's source.

The fourth column of the index cites American collections published after 1761 whose settings resemble those in *Urania* so closely that *Urania* seems likely to have been the compiler's source. To save space, only the compiler and the date appear; the collections are fully identified at the end of the index. Only a tune's first appearance in a given collection is noted, and no attempt has been made to list printings in subsequent editions of the same work. The information on American printings of the tunes in *Urania* is based on the author's unpublished thematic index of American tunebooks, 1698–1810.

Finally, the blank spaces in the Index of Compositions deserve some explanation. All blanks in the second or third columns represent desiderata and should be interpreted as question marks—except those following compositions identified as first printings. A blank in the fourth column means that the tune was printed in America after *Urania* but that I have found no setting of it which corresponds with Lyon's.

INDEX OF COMPOSITIONS

Tune and Composer	First Publication	Lyon's Probable Source	Later American Publications of Setting Resembling Lyon's
ANGELS HYMN[1] by Gibbons	Wither, *Hymnes*, 1623 (Frost *HC*)	Ashworth, *Collection*, c. 1760	Law, 1781; Jocelin, 1782; *Sacred Harmony*, 1788; Adgate, 1789; Shumway, 1793; Read, 1794
BATH		Ashworth, *Collection*, c. 1760	Adgate, 1789
BEDFORD by Wheal	Timbrell, *Guide*, before 1723 (Frost *HC*)		*Tunes*, 1763; Law, 1781; *Sacred Harmony*, 1788; Adgate, 1789; Shumway, 1793
BRUNSWICK[2]			*Tunes*, 1763; Hopkinson, 1763; *Sacred Harmony*, 1788; Adgate, 1789
CANTERBURY	Este, *Psalms*, 1592 (Frost *E&S* 19)	Arnold, *Compleat Psalmodist*, 1756	Adgate, 1791
CHRISTMAS HYMN[3] by Palma	1st pr.		*Sacred Harmony*, 1788; Benjamin, 1799
COLESHILL[4]	Smith, *Psalms*, c. 1698 (Frost *E&S* 392a)		*Tunes*, 1763; Hopkinson, 1763; Law, 1783; *Sacred Harmony*, 1788; Adgate, 1789
COOKFIELD		Adams, *Companion*, c. 1760; Evison, *Compleat Book*, 1751	[no later printings]
CRANLEY		Arnold, *Compleat Psalmodist*, 1756	[no later printings]
CROWLE	Green, *Psalm-Tunes*, 1724 (Frost *HC*)	Ashworth, *Collection*, c. 1760	*Tunes*, 1763
DAGENHAM		Arnold, *Compleat Psalmodist*, 1756	Flagg, 1766
DARKING		Adams, *Companion*, c. 1760; Evison, *Compleat Book*, 1751	[no later printings]
DERBY[5]	*New Method*, 1686 (*Hymns A&M*)	Turner, *Tunes*, 1752	*Tunes*, 1763; *Sacred Harmony*, 1788

Tune and Composer	First Publication	Lyon's Probable Source	Later American Publications of Setting Resembling Lyon's
DORCHESTER	Knapp, *Sett*, 1738	Arnold, *Compleat Psalmodist*, 1756; Evison, *Compleat Book*, 1751	[no later printings]
GLOUCESTER	Ravenscroft, *Whole Book*, 1621 (Frost *E&S* 239)		Read, 1794
HALLELUJAH		*Harmonia Sacra*, c. 1760	*Sacred Harmony*, 1788
ISLE OF WIGHT	Browne, *Sett*, c. 1720 (Lowens)		*Tunes*, 1763; Jocelin, 1788; *Sacred Harmony*, 1788; Adgate, 1789
ITALIAN		*Harmonia Sacra*, c. 1760	*Sacred Harmony*, 1788
JUDGMENT			*Sacred Harmony*, 1788
KETTERING	Sheeles, *Skylark*, c. 1740 (Frost *HC*)	*Divine Musical Miscellany*, 1754	*Sacred Harmony*, 1788
KETTLEBY'S		*Harmonia Sacra*, c. 1760	Bayley, 1784
LEATHERED		Adams, *Companion*, c. 1760; Evison, *Compleat Book*, 1751	[no later printings]
LONDON NEW	*Psalms*, 1635 (Frost *E&S* 222)		Adgate, 1791
MEAR	Browne, *Sett*, c. 1720 (Lowens)		*Tunes*, 1763; Hopkinson, 1763; Law, 1781; Jocelin, 1788; *Sacred Harmony*, 1788; Adgate, 1789; Shumway, 1793; Read, 1794
MORNING HYMN			*Tunes*, 1763; Flagg, 1764; Bayley, 1769; Stickney, 1774; *Sacred Harmony*, 1788; Adgate, 1789
NEWCASTLE[6]			*Tunes*, 1763; Jocelin, 1782; *Sacred Harmony*, 1788

Tune and Composer	First Publication	Lyon's Probable Source	Later American Publications of Setting Resembling Lyon's
ORANGE		Ashworth, *Collection*, c. 1760	Law, 1783
PALMY'S		*Harmonia Sacra*, c. 1760	Law, 1783a
PORTSMOUTH	Browne, *Sett*, c. 1720 (Lowens)	Johnston, *Tunes*, 1755; Walter, *Grounds*, 1760	Jocelin, 1782; *Sacred Harmony*, 1788
PSALM 4			*Sacred Harmony*, 1788; Benjamin, 1799
PSALM 5[7]		Adams, *Companion*, c. 1760	Jocelin, 1782; *Sacred Harmony*, 1788
PSALM 8 by Lyon	1st pr. (Lyon)		[no later printings]
PSALM 9[8] by Tuckey	1st pr.		Jocelin, 1782
PSALM 12[9]		Adams, *Companion*, c. 1760	[no later printings]
PSALM 15	Arnold, *Leicestershire Harmony*, 1759	Arnold, *Leicestershire*, 1759	Bayley, 1773; Stickney, 1774; Law, 1783
PSALM 23[10] by Hopkinson	1st pr. (Lyon)		Hopkinson, 1763; Stickney, 1774
PSALM 33[11] by Tuckey	1st pr.		Law, 1779; Jocelin, 1782; *Sacred Harmony*, 1788; Adgate, 1791
PSALM 40 by Smith	Smith, *Set*, c. 1750	Smith, *Set*, c. 1750	[no later printings]
PSALM 43 by Smith	Smith, *Set*, c. 1750	Smith, *Set*, c. 1750	[no later printings]
PSALM 50 New		Ashworth, *Collection*, c. 1760	*Tunes*, 1763; Law, 1781
PSALM 50 Old	*Anglo-Genevan Psalter*, 1558 (Frost *E&S* 69)	Ashworth, *Collection*, c. 1760	*Sacred Harmony*, 1788; Adgate, 1789

Tune and Composer	First Publication	Lyon's Probable Source	Later American Publications of Setting Resembling Lyon's
PSALM 56		Holdroyd, *Companion*, 1753	[no later printings]
PSALM 57		Arnold, *Compleat Psalmodist*, 1756	Jocelin, 1782; Law, 1783
PSALM 90[12]	Arnold, *Leicestershire Harmony*, 1759	Arnold, *Leicestershire*, 1759	Law, 1781; Jocelin, 1782; Benjamin, 1799
PSALM 95 by Lyon	1st pr. (Lyon)		[no later printings]
PSALM 98		Green, *Psalmody*, 1734	*Tunes*, 1763; *Sacred Harmony*, 1788
PSALM 100 NEW[13]	Tufts, *Introduction*, 1723 (Lowens)	Tufts, *Introduction*, 1726; Johnston, *Tunes*, 1755; Walter, *Grounds*, 1760	*Sacred Harmony*, 1788; Adgate, 1791; Shumway, 1793
PSALM 100 OLD	Bourgeois, *Genevan Psalter*, 1551 (Frost *HC*)		Jocelin, 1782; *Sacred Harmony*, 1788; Adgate, 1789; Shumway, 1793
PSALM 102[14]		Davenport, *Pocket Companion*, 1758	Law, 1781; Jocelin, 1782
PSALM 112	Schumann, *Geistliche Lieder*, 1539 (Frost *HC*)		*Tunes*, 1763
PSALM 113 NEW[15] by Holdroyd		Holdroyd, *Companion*, 1753	[no later printings]
PSALM 113 OLD	*Anglo-Genevan Psalter*, 1561 (Frost *E&S* 125)	Arnold, *Compleat Psalmodist*, 1756	
PSALM 119 NEW		Davenport, *Pocket Companion*, 1758	[no later printings]
PSALM 119 OLD	*Anglo-Genevan Psalter*, 1558 (Frost *E&S* 132)	Turner, *Tunes*, 1752; Johnston, *Tunes*, 1755	
PSALM 122 NEW			
PSALM 136		Johnston, *Tunes*, 1755; Arnold, *Compleat Psalmodist*, 1756	

Tune and Composer	First Publication	Lyon's Probable Source	Later American Publications of Setting Resembling Lyon's
PSALM 145[16]	Arnold, *Leicestershire Harmony*, 1759	Arnold, *Leicestershire*, 1759	Jocelin, 1782; Law, 1783
PSALM 148			[no later printings]
PSALM 148 OLD	*Anglo-Genevan Psalter*, 1558 (Frost *E&S* 174)	Ashworth, *Collection*, c. 1760	
PSALM 149[17]	*Supplement*, 1708 (Frost *HC*)	Ashworth, *Collection*, c. 1760	Adgate, 1789
PSALM 150[18]		Adams, *Companion*, c. 1760	Law, 1779; Jocelin, 1782
PUBLIC WORSHIP		*Harmonia Sacra*, c. 1760	
RESURRECTION[19]		*Divine Musical Miscellany*, 1754	Benjamin, 1799
RIPON[20] by Barrow		Arnold, *Compleat Psalmodist*, 1756	Tan'sur, 1767; Williams, 1769
RYGATE[21] by Evison		Adams, *Companion*, c. 1760; Evison, *Compleat Book*, 1751	[no later printings]
ST. ANN'S by Croft	*Supplement*, 1708 (Frost *HC*)		Adgate, 1791
ST. DAVID'S	Ravenscroft, *Whole Book*, 1621 (Frost *E&S* 234)	Arnold, *Compleat Psalmodist*, 1756	
ST. HUMPHREY'S		Turner, *Tunes*, 1752	*Tunes*, 1763; Hopkinson, 1763; *Sacred Harmony*, 1788; Adgate, 1789
ST. MATTHEW'S (Hymn)	*Supplement*, 1708 (Frost *HC*)	*Harmonia Sacra*, c. 1760	
ST. MATTHEW'S		Adams, *Companion*, c. 1760	Law, 1781
ST. MICHAEL'S[22]	Holdroyd, *Companion*, c. 1724 (Lightwood)	Ashworth, *Collection*, c. 1760	Adgate, 1789; Shumway, 1793

Tune and Composer	First Publication	Lyon's Probable Source	Later American Publications of Setting Resembling Lyon's
ST. PETER'S	Playford, *Whole Book*, 1677 (Frost *E&S* 154b)	Ashworth, *Collection*, c. 1760	*Tunes*, 1763
SALISBURY[23]	*Lyra Davidica*, 1708 (Frost *HC*)		Aitken, 1787; *Sacred Harmony*, 1788
SKY LARK		*Harmonia Sacra*, c. 1760	Law, 1783a
SOUTHWELL	Daman, *Psalms*, 1579 (Frost *E&S* 65)	Ashworth, *Collection*, c. 1760	*Tunes*, 1763
STANDISH	*Psalm-Singer's Companion*, 1700 (Lowens)	Turner, *Tunes*, 1752; Johnston, *Tunes*, 1755	Law, 1783; *Sacred Harmony*, 1788; Adgate, 1789
WALSALL	Anchors, *Collection*, c. 1721 (Frost *HC*)	Ashworth, *Collection*, c. 1760	Law, 1783; Adgate, 1791
WATT'S[24] by Lyon	1st pr. (Lyon)		*Tunes*, 1763; Hopkinson, 1763; Aitken, 1787; Adgate, 1791
WELLS[25] by Holdroyd		Ashworth, *Collection*, c. 1760	
WESTMINSTER	Playford, *Whole Book*, 1677 (Frost *E&S* 362c)	Arnold, *Compleat Psalmodist*, 1756	Hopkinson, 1763
WHITEFIELD'S[26]	*Thesaurus Musicus*, 1744		*Sacred Harmony*, 1788
WILLINGTON			*Tunes*, 1763; Jocelin, 1782; Law, 1783; *Sacred Harmony*, 1788
WINDSOR	Daman, *Psalms*, 1591 (Frost *E&S* 129)	Arnold, *Compleat Psalmodist*, 1756	Shumway, 1793
WIRKSWORTH[27]	Chetham, *Psalmody*, 1718 (Frost *HC*)	Ashworth, *Collection*, c. 1760	*Tunes*, 1763; Adgate, 1789

ANTHEMS

I will bless the Lord[28]	Arnold, *Leicestershire Harmony*, 1759	Arnold, *Leicestershire*, 1759	[no later printings]

Tune and Composer	First Publication	Lyon's Probable Source	Later American Publications of Setting Resembling Lyon's
I will magnify[29] by Townshend		Arnold, *Compleat Psalmodist*, 1756	[no later printings]
Is there not an appointed time[30]		Adams, *Companion*, c. 1760	Bayley, 1773; Stickney, 1774; Law, 1779
Jehovah reigns[31] by Tuckey	1st pr.		Stickney, 1774
Let the shrill trumpet's	1st pr. (Lyon)		Bayley, 1769; Stickney, 1774; Benjamin, 1799
O be joyful[32]		Davenport, *Pocket Companion*, 1758	[no later printings]
O clap your hands[33]		Davenport, *Pocket Companion*, 1758	[no later printings]
O give thanks			[no later printings]
O praise the Lord			[no later printings]
O sing unto the Lord[34]		Davenport, *Pocket Companion*, 1758	[no later printings]
Preserve me O God[35]		Adams, *Companion*, c. 1760	Jocelin, 1788
The Lord descended by Lyon	1st pr. (Lyon)		

COLLECTIONS NAMED IN SOURCE COLUMN

Adams, Abraham. *The Psalmist's New Companion.* 6th edition. London: Thompson & son, c.1760.

Arnold, John. *The Compleat Psalmodist.* 4th edition. London: Robert Brown, 1756.

———. *The Leicestershire Harmony.* London: Robert Brown for the author, 1759.

Ashworth, Caleb. *A Collection of Tunes.* London: J. Buckland, c.1760.

Davenport, Uriah. *The Psalm-Singer's Pocket Companion.* 2nd edition. London: Robert Brown, 1758.

The Divine Musical Miscellany. London: Wm. Smith, 1754.

Evison, James. *A Compleat Book of Psalmody.* 2nd edition. London: Robert Brown, 1751.

Green, James. *A Book of Psalmody.* 8th edition. London: W. Pearson for the author, 1734.

Harmonia Sacra. London: for Thomas Butts, c.1760.

Holdroyd, Israel. *The Spiritual Man's Companion.* 5th edition. London: Robert Brown, 1753.

Smith, John. *A Set of Services, Anthems & Psalm Tunes.* London: for the Author, c.1750.

Tufts, John. *An Introduction to the Singing of Psalm-Tunes.* 5th edition. Boston: for Samuel Gerrish, 1726.

[*Tunes.*] Boston: engraved, printed, and sold by Thomas Johnston, 1755.

[*Tunes.*] Boston: engraved, printed, and sold by James A. Turner, 1752.

Walter, Thomas. *The Grounds and Rules of Musick.* Boston: Benjamin Mecom, 1760. (This was either the 5th or 6th edition.)

LATER AMERICAN COLLECTIONS CITED IN INDEX

Adgate, 1789   Adgate, Andrew. *Philadelphia Harmony.* Philadelphia: for the author, [1789].

Adgate, 1791   Adgate, Andrew. *Philadelphia Harmony, Part II.* Philadelphia: [John M'Culloch, 1791].

Aitken, 1787   Aitken, John. *A Compilation of the Litanies and Vespers Hymns and Anthems.* Philadelphia, 1787.

Bayley, 1769   Bayley, Daniel. *The American Harmony.* (Containing William Tans'ur, *Royal Melody Compleat,* and Aaron Williams, *Universal Psalmodist.*) Newburyport: the author, 1769.

Bayley, 1773   ———. *The New Universal Harmony.* Newburyport: the author, 1773.

Bayley, 1784   ———. *Select Harmony.* Newburyport: the author, 1784.

Benjamin, 1799   Benjamin, Jonathan. *Harmonia Coelestis.* Northampton: Andrew Wright for O. D. & I. Cooke, 1799.

Flagg, 1764   Flagg, Josiah. *A Collection of the Best Psalm Tunes.* Boston: Paul Revere & the author, 1764.

Flagg, 1766   ———. *Sixteen Anthems.* Boston: the author, [1766].

Hopkinson, 1763   [Hopkinson, Francis.] *A Collection of Psalm Tunes.* Philadelphia, 1763.

Jocelin, 1782   [Jocelin, Simeon, and Amos Doolittle.] *The Chorister's Companion.* New Haven: the author & Amos Doolittle, [1782].

Jocelin, 1788   [Jocelin, Simeon.] *The Chorister's Companion.* 2nd edition. New Haven: the author & Amos Doolittle, 1788.

Law, 1779   Law, Andrew. *Select Harmony.* [Cheshire: William Law], 1779.

Law, 1781   ———. *A Select Number of Plain Tunes.* [Cheshire: William Law, 1781.]

Law, 1783   ———. *The Rudiments of Music.* [Cheshire: William Law,] 1783.

Law, 1783a   ———. *A Collection of Hymn Tunes.* Cheshire: Wm. Law, [1783].

Read, 1794   Read, Daniel. *The Columbian Harmonist, No. 2.* New Haven: the author, [1794].

Sacred Harmony, 1788   *A Selection of Sacred Harmony.* Philadelphia: John M'Culloch, 1788.

Shumway, 1793   Shumway, Nehemiah. *The American Harmony.* Philadelphia: John M'Culloch, 1793.

Stickney, 1774   Stickney, John. *The Gentleman and Lady's Musical Companion.* Newburyport: Daniel Bayley, 1774.

Tan'sur, 1767   Tan'sur, William. *The Royal Melody Complete,* 3rd edition. Boston: William M'Alpine, 1767.

Tunes, 1763   *Tunes in Three Parts.* Philadelphia: Anthony Armbruster, 1763.

FOOTNOTES FOR APPENDIX II

[1] ANGELS HYMN is printed as ANGEL'S SONG in Ashworth's *Collection*.

[2] British hymnological sources do not establish the date of the first printing of BRUNSWICK, but c.1720 is a strong possibility. Simon Browne's *Sett of Tunes*, c.1720, contained the tune under the title DORCHESTER, and William Anchors, *Choice Collection*, c.1725, printed it with an attribution to "S. Brown."

[3] Palma's authorship was established by Robert Stevenson. See Stevenson, *Protestant Church Music in America* (New York: Norton, 1966), 46–47.

[4] COLESHILL appeared in Law's collection as DUBLIN.

[5] DERBY appeared in Turner's collection as BELLA.

[6] Sonneck discovered a three-voice setting of NEWCASTLE in Williams's *Universal Psalmodist* (1763) which corresponds closely with Lyon's treble, tenor, and bass. But the date of Williams's collection rules it out as Lyon's source. A logical conclusion is that Lyon and Williams drew upon the same British source, a work whose identity is yet to be discovered.

[7] PSALM 5 appeared in Adams's collection as CUDHAM. Both Jocelin and Adgate printed it under the title NEWBURY.

[8] PSALM 9 was attributed to Tuckey in the second edition of Jocelin's collection (1788).

[9] PSALM 12 appeared in Adams's collection as WROTHAM.

[10] The attribution to Hopkinson was established by Robert Stevenson. See his *Protestant Church Music in America*, 47.

[11] PSALM 33 was attributed to Tuckey in Jocelin's collection.

[12] PSALM 90 appeared in Benjamin's collection as WALTHAM.

[13] The melody of PSALM 100 NEW may have been printed in Tufts's *Introduction* of 1721, but that edition is lost. The earliest discovered extant printing is a two-voice setting in the third edition of 1723. See Theodore M. Finney, "The Third Edition of Tufts' *Introduction to the Art of Singing Psalm-Tunes*," *Journal of Research in Music Education*, XIV/3 (Fall 1966), 169. See also Lowens, *Music and Musicians*, 53–55. Though Lowens had not seen the third edition when he wrote his article, Finney found nothing to contradict Lowens's conclusion that PSALM 100 NEW was composed in America.

[14] PSALM 102 appeared in Law's and Jocelin's collections as PARINDON.

[15] The attribution to Holdroyd is taken from Crisp, *Divine Harmony* (1755), where PSALM 113 NEW appears as ST. JAMES.

[16] PSALM 145 was published in Arnold's collection as COATES, a setting of Psalm 23. Andrew Law published it as KENSINGTON.

[17] PSALM 149 appeared as PSALM 104 in Ashworth's collection. Frost *HC* lists it as HANOVER.

[18] PSALM 150 appeared as SHOREHAM in Adams's collection.

[19] RESURRECTION appeared in Benjamin's collection as WALTHAM.

[20] The attribution to Barrow is taken from his *Psalm-Singer's Choice Companion* (3rd edition, c.1760).

[21] Evison's *Compleat Book* (1751) contains the attribution.

[22] ST. MICHAEL'S appeared in Adgate's and Shumway's collections as ROCHESTER.

[23] SALISBURY appeared in Aitken's collection as SING YE PRAISES. Frost *HC* lists it as EASTER HYMN.

[24] WATTS'S appeared in *Tunes* as LYON, in Hopkinson's *Collection* as HYMN, and in Aitken's and Adgate's works as PSALM 104.

[25] The attribution of WELLS to Holdroyd was traditional in eighteenth-century American collections. The tune does appear without a title in the first edition of Holdroyd's *Spiritual-Man's Companion* (c.1724) as a setting of Psalm 100.

[26] Percy A. Scholes made a detailed study of this tune, a slightly-altered version of the British National Anthem, "God save the Queen." A summary of his study appears in the *Oxford Companion to Music*, 9th edition (London: Oxford University Press, 1955), 410–16. Scholes found melodies resembling it in early seventeenth-century sources, but he gives the *Thesaurus Musicus* as the source where it first appeared in a form close to the one Lyon printed.

[27] WIRKSWORTH appeared in Adgate's collection as AYLESBURY.

[28] Arnold's index lists the work under its text source, Psalm 34.

[29] The attribution to Nathaniel Townshend is taken from Crisp, *Divine Harmony* (1755).

[30] Adams's index lists the work under its text source, Job 7.

[31] The attribution to Tuckey was made by Andrew Adgate. See Sonneck, *Early Concert-Life*, 108.

[32] Davenport's index lists the work under its text source, Psalm 100.

[33] Davenport's index lists the work under its text source, Psalm 47.

[34] Davenport's index lists the work under its text source, Psalm 96.

[35] Adams's index lists the work under its text source, Psalm 16.

URANIA

URANIA,

or

A Choice Collection of Psalm-Tunes, Anthems, and Hymns

From the most approv'd Authors, with some Entirely New;

in Two, Three, and Four, Parts

Thewhole Peculiarly adapted to the Use of

CHURCHES, and PRIVATE FAMILIES.

To which are Prefix'd

The Plainest, & most Necessary Rules of Psalmody.

By JAMES LYON, A.B.

Hen Dawkins Fecit 1761

TO

The Clergy of every Denomination

in *America.*

Reverend Sirs,

RELYING on the evident Propriety of your patronizing this Publication, permit me to lay Urania at your Feet.

Should the following Collection of Tunes be so fortunate, as to merit your Approbation; To please the Taste of the Public; To assist the private Christian in his daily Devotion; And to improve, in any Degree, an important Part of Divine Service in these Colonies, for which it

was

was defigned : I fhall think myfelf happy in being the Editor, notwithftanding the great Expence, Labour, and Anxiety, it has coft me to compleat it.

MAY You long continue Ornaments of your Profeffion: Daily fee abundant Fruits of your Labour in the Reformation of Mankind : And inceffantly enjoy thofe fublime Pleafures, which nothing, but a Series of rational and virtuous Actions, can create.

I am,
Reverend Gentlemen,
Your moft obedient,
and humble Servant,

J A M E S   L Y O N.

The INDEX.

* All Tunes marked with an Asterism are New.

SUBSCRIBERS NAMES.

A.

REV. Francis Alison, D. D. *Vice-Provost of the College and Academy of Philadelphia.*

Joseph Alexander, A. B. Naf.

John Archer, A. B. Naf.

Mr. Joseph Arthur.

Miss S. Aris.

Miss P. Aris.

Mr. William Ayers.

B.

Jonathan Baldwin, A. M. *Steward of Naffau-Hall in New Jersey,* 6 Books.

Abfalom Bambrage, *Student of N. H.*

Mr. Andrew Bankfon, *Merchant.*

Mr. John Barnes, jun.

Mr. George Baxter.

Mr. John Bayard, *Merchant.*

Rev. Mr. Beaty.

Mr. John Bleakly.

Capt. Thomas Bourne.

Dr. John Boyd.

Mr. William Bradford, 2 Books.

Rev. Mr. John Brainerd.

Miss S. Budden.

Andrew Burr, *Esq;* 2 Books.

David Burr, *Esq,*

Mr. Thaddeus Burr, *Merchant* of *New England*

C.

Rev. Mr. James Caldwell.

Rev. Mr. John Carmichael.

Mr. Daniel Cartrite.

Miss H. Chambers.

Mr. Thomas Charlton.

Mr. James Child, *Merchant,* 4 Books.

John Clark, A. B. Naf.

James Clark, *Student of N. H.*

Miss Ann Clarkfon.

Mrs. Elizabeth Clemm.

John Clofe, *Student* of N. H.

Mr. Daniel Cunyngham Clymer, *Student of N. H.*

Mr. Charles Cox, *Merchant,* 3 Books.

D.

Rev. Mr. Samuel Davies, *Prefident of Naffau-Hall in New-Jerfey deceafed,* 4 Books.

Jofiah F. Davenport, *Esq;* 2 Books.

Edmund Davis, *Student of N. H.*

Mr. Andrew Doz, *Merchant.*

Elijah Dwight, *Stuent* of N. H.

Mr. John Dupliffis.

E.

Rev. Mr. John Ewing.

Mr. Ofwell Eve, *Merchant.*

F.

Mr. James Faris, 6 Books.

Rev. Mr. Samuel Finley, *Prefident of Naffau Hall in New Jerfey.*

Mr. John Fullerton, 2 Books.

G.

Edward Gantt, *Student of N. H.*

Miss E. Greame.

Mrs.

Mrs. Mary Grant, 2 Books.

Enoch Green, A. B. Naf.

Rev. Mr. Nehemiah Greenman.

H.

Jeremiah Halfey, M. A. *Tutor of Naffau Hall, in New-Jerfey.*

Robert Halftead, *Student of N. H,*

John Harris, *Student of N H,*

Mr. Hellings,

Mr. Memucan Hughes,

Rev. Mr. James Hunt, *of Virginia,*

Mafter Hunt, *of Antigua,*

Rev. Mr. Andrew Hunter,

John Huntington, A. B. *Naf. of Norwick New England,*

I.

Samuel Jones, *Student of the College in Philadelphia.*

K.

Enos Kelfy, A. B. Naf.

Jacob Kerr, A. B. *Tutor of Naffau Hall in New Jerfey,* 2 Books,

L.

Rev. Mr. Daniel Lawrence,

Mr. John Leacock,

Mr. Livingfworth, *of Waterberry New England,*

John Lothrop, *Student of N. H.*

Mr. Henry Loughhead, *of Chefter County,* 3 Books,

Mr. James Loughhead,

Nehemiah Ludlum, *Student of N. H.*

Mr. Henry Lyon, *of Newark New Jerfey,*

M.

Mr. Eleazar M'Combs, Merchant in New-York,

Mr. Hugh M'Cullough,

Mr. John M'Crea,

James Maning, *Student of N. H.* 2 Books,

Mr. John Meafe,

John Dyer Mercier, *Student of N. H.*

Jofeph Merfhon, *Student of N. H.* 2 Books,

Mr. Andrew Merfhon,

William Mills, A. M. *of Long Ifland,*

N.

Obadiah Noble, *Student of N. H.*

O.

Robert Ogden, *Student of N. H.*

P.

Mr. Charles Pettit, Merchant, 3 Books,

Mifs S. Parker,

Mr. Arthur Parks, *of New York,*

William Patterfon, *Student of N. H.*

Mr. George Plater, 2 Books,

Mr. Powell,

Dr. B. Youngs Prime, *of Long Ifland,*

R.

Mr. John Ralfton, *at the Forks of Delaware,*

Rev. Mr. William Ramfey,

James

SUBSCRIBERS NAMES.

James Read, *Esq; of Reading,* 12 Books,

Mr. Joseph Redman, Merchant,

Andrew Reed, *Esq;* 2 Books,

Mr. James Reid,

Mr. John Reily,

Mr. John Rhea, Merchant, 4 Books,

Daniel Roberdeau, Esq; 5 Books,

Mr. Thomas Robinson, *of Burlington,*

Rev. Mr. John Rodgers, 3 Books,

Mr. William Rush,

Benjamin Rush, A. B. Naf.

S.

Mr. John Sayre, 2 Books,

Mr. William Sellers.

Eraftus Sergeant, *Student of N. H.*

Jonathan Sergeant, *Student of N. H.*

Henry Sherburne, jun. A. B. of *Portfmouth Newhampfhire,*

Dr. William Shippen, 3 Books,

Mr. James Small, *of Somerfet County Maryland,*

Rev. William Smith, D. D. *Provoft of the College and Academy of Philadelphia,* 4 Books,

Mr. Samuel Smith, Merchant,

Rev. Mr. Robert Smith, *of Pequay,*

Jonathan Smith, A. B. Naf.

Mr. Jedediah Snowden,

Mr. Ilaic Snowden, 2 Books,

Mr. Thomas Stamper,

Mr. Valentine Standley, 2 Books,

Mr. Ifaac Stretch,

Mr. William Symonds, Merchant,

Mr. Philip Syng, 2 Books,

T.

Mr. Benjamin Taylor,

Josiah Thatcher, A. B. Naf. *of New England,*

Amos Thomson, A. B. Naf. *of New England,*

James Thomson, *Student of N. H.*

Mr. Giles Tidmarsh,

Rev. Mr. Jonathan Todd, *of Virginia,* 4 Books,

Joseph Treat, A. M. *Tutor of N. H.*

U.

Mr. Robert Ufher, Merchant,

Mr. Vanderfpreigel, Merchant,

Lawrence Vanderveer, *Student of N. H.*

W.

Mr. John Wallace, 2 Books,

Mr. Joseph Watkins,

Mr. White, Merchant, 3 Books,

Mr. Thomas White,

Mr. Henry Williams,

Edmund Winfton, *Student of N. H.*

Mr. John Wood, 3 Books.

Mr. Joseph Woodruff, *of New York,*

Mr. Jeremiah Wool,

Y.

Mr. William Young, 2 Books.

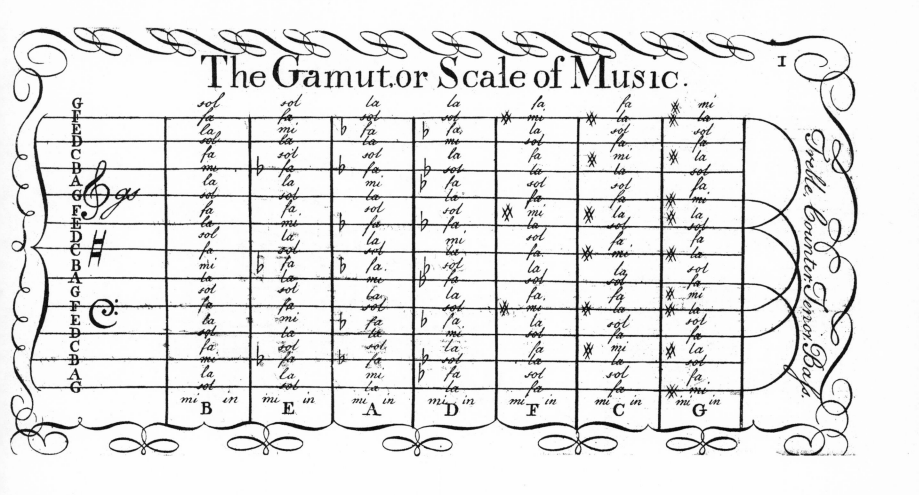

II

The Four parts Separate.

sol. la. fa. sol. la. mi. fa. sol. la. fa. sol.

la. fa. sol. la. mi. fa. sol. la. fa. sol. la.

fa. sol. la. fa. sol. la. mi. fa. sol. la. fa.

fa. sol. la. mi. fa. sol. la. fa. sol. la. mi.

A Scale of Notes and their Proportions.

1 Semibreve   Contains

2 Minims   Contains

4 Crotchets   Contains

8 Quavers   Contains

16 Semiquavers   Contains

32   Demisemiqu.

N.B. the Notes bear the same Proportion to each other in all sorts of time.

Explanation of the Gamut.

The 4 Parts of Music are distinguished from one another by 4 Semicircles, each including 5 Lines with their Proper Cliffs and Letters. The first is the Bass, or lowest Part in Music, and known by the **F** Cliff which always stands on **F**. The 2ᵈ is the Tenor, with the **C** Cliff on **C** its 4ᵗʰ Line. The 3ᵈ is Counter with the **C** Cliff on **C**, its 3ᵈ Line: And the 4ᵗʰ is Treble, the highest part of Music, with the **G** Cliff on **G**, its 2ᵈ Line. The **F** & **G** Cliffs in most Authors are immovable, but when they move, the Letters which are the Names of the Lines and Spaces, always move with them, in the same order as they stand in the Gamut. The **C** Cliff is movable in all Authors, but the Line it stands on is always **C**, and must be sounded a 5ᵗʰ above the **F** Cliff, and a 5ᵗʰ below the **G** Cliff, except when the latter is prefix'd to a part design'd for mens Voices (which is frequently the case with the Tenor & Counter in this Book) then it is a 4ᵗʰ above the **G** Cliff, for that is now an Octave (or 8 Notes) below its usual place, and Unison (or the same sound) with the highest **G** in the Bass.

IV. The four Monosyllables sol. la, mi, fa. Seldom change the Order in which they stand in the Gamut: viz. from mi. to mi ascending they are fa, sol, la, fa. sol. la. &. descending la, sol, fa, la, sol, fa; And the two Semitones or half Notes in every Octave are invariably fix'd between mi & fa, & la & fa, throughout all the Removes of mi, except when a Flat. Sharp, or Natural, is plac'd immediately before some particular Note. All Notes upon Lines & Spaces, not mark'd with either Flats or Sharps, are call'd Natural Notes, & are represented by the Monosyllables in the 2.d Column of the Gamut. In all the succeeding Columns, they are remov'd to other Letters by Flats & Sharps, according to the following Rules, but in such a manner, that they express those Flats & Sharps, without affecting any of the Natural Notes.

1. When neither a Flat nor Sharp is set at the Beginning of a Tune. Mi is in B. But,

2. If B. be flat, Mi is in E. ———

3. If B. & E. be flat, Mi is in A. ———

4. If B. E. & A. be flat, Mi is in D. ———

5. If B. E. A. & D. be flat, Mi is in G. ———

6. If F. be Sharp, Mi is in F. ———

7. If F. & C. be Sharp, Mi is in C. ———

8. If F. C. & G. be Sharp, Mi is in G. ———

9. If F. C. G. & D. be Sharp, Mi is in D. ———

Of Time, or the Duration of Sounds in Music.

Time is of two Kinds, viz. Common, & Triple, in one or the other of which all Movements are included. Common Time is measured by an even Number of Beats in each Bar, the first half of which must be perform'd with the Hand or Foot down, & the other with it up; Its first Mood is a very slow & grave Mobement, containing one Semibreve, or its Quantity in every Bar, which ought to be sounded about 4 Seconds, or while you may leisurely say 1. 2. 3. 4. This Mood is mark'd thus.

The 2d. Mood has a line drawn thro' the C ℭ & should be sung about half as fast again as the first. The 3d. Mood is known by a C. inverted Ɔ from which it is called the Retortive Mood, or by a Figure of Two 2 And must be sung as quick again as the first Mood. The last Mood worthy of Notice in this Place is Mark'd thus 2/4 & called 2 to 4 containing one Minim or two Crotchets &c. in a Bar, which require nearly the same Time that y e same Notes require in the 2d. Mood. In beating the 2 first of these Moods the Hand should have 4 equiable Motions in every Bar, 2 down & 2 up. And in the 2. last Mood only 2 Motions, one down and the other up: According to the following Examples in Common Time, where d is put for down, & u for up: and the Number of Beats in each

Bar

VI Bar shewn by an equal Number of Figures, directly over them.

Triple Time is known by the following Characters $\frac{3}{2}$ $\frac{3}{4}$ $\frac{3}{8}$ the first of which contains 3 Minims in a Bar, which ought to be sung in the Time of 2 Minims, in the first Mood of Common Time. The 2.ᵈ contains 3 Crotchets in a Bar, which are sung about as quick as Crotchets, in the 2.ᵈ Mood of Common Time. The last contains 3 Quavers in a Bar, which are sung as quick as Crotchets in Retortive Time. Each Bar in Triple Time, whether quick or slow, is divided into three equal Parts, the two first of which must be perform'd with the Hand or Foot down, & the last with it up. according to the following Examples.

Example of Rests.

Semibreve Rest. Minim Rest. Crotchet Rest. Quaver R. Semiq. R. Demisemiq R. 2 Bars. 3 Bars. 4 Bars. 8 Bars.

Rests.
Notes.

Note. A Semibreve Rest is a whole Bar in any Time whatever.

A Single Bar divides the Time according to the measure Note. A Double Bar divides every Strain or Part of a Tune, & shows the End of the Lines in Psalm & Hymn Tunes. A Repeat signifies that such a Part of a Tune, from the Note over or before which it is put, must be sung over again. A Hold or Pause signifies that the Note, over which it is plac'd, must be sounded something longer than its usual Time; it also denotes the End of a Tune. A Direct is put at the End of the Lines, when broke off by the Narrowness of the Paper, to show the Place of the first Note in the succeeding Lines. A Slur or Tye drawn over or under any Quantity of Notes signifies, that they are all to be sung to one Syllable. Three Crotchets with a Figure of 3 over or under them must be sung in the Time of a Minim; & three Quavers in the Time of a Crotchet &c.

Of Flats Sharps & Naturals.

A Flat ♭ placed before any Note signifies that, that Note (and all on the same Letter in that Bar, except mark'd to the contrary) must be sung a Semitone lower than its Natural Pitch. The Sharp ♯ is of a contrary Nature, and raises a Note a Semitone higher than its Natural Sound. When Flats are set at the Beginning of a Tune, they affect all the Notes on the same Letters, on which they stand, thro' the whole Movement; thus if a Flat be set on B, B must be sounded half a Note lower than its Natural Pitch, thro' the Tune, unless the Flat is removed by a Sharp or Natural. Sharps set at the Beginning of a Tune have the contrary Effect. A Natural ♮ reduces any Note, made flat or sharp by the governing Flats or Sharps in the Beginning of a Tune, to its primitive Sound.

Of the Keys in Music.

The Letter, on which a Tune closes, is called its Key, which is known to be either flat or Sharp by the third above the last Note in the Bass; if that third contains two whole Tones, the Tune is on a sharp Key, but if only a Tone & Semitone, it is a flat Key.

Of Syncopation.

All Notes placed in such a Part of the Bar, that they require the Hand to be taken up, or put down, while they are sounding; or divided by a single Bar, as in this Example are call'd Notes of Syncopation. Note, they are also called driving Notes.

Of Transposition.

When a Tune happens to be on a wrong Key, either too high or too low, it may be transpos'd or removed to any other Key, by adding Flats or Sharps, or by omitting them, as Occasion requires. But great Care must be taken, that the Notes retain their old Names, & bear the same Relation to each other, as before; and that all accidental Flats & Sharps are inserted, unless Naturals will answer the End better.

The above Example shews how the same Tune may be transpos'd, not only from **G to C**; or from **C to G**: But to any other of the 7 Letters. Example of pointed Notes! A Dot on the right side of a Note makes it half as long again. Thus one Semibreve is equal to 3 Minims &c.

Of the Graces in Music.

Trill. Explain'd. Beat. Explain'd. Forefall. Expl. Backfall. Expl. Turn Expl. Shake turn'd Expl. Grace of Transition.

The Trill or Shake is used on all descending prickt Crotchets; on the latter of two Notes on the same Line or Space; and generally before a Close. The other Graces are seldom used in plain Church-Tunes, but are very proper in Hymns & Anthems. Note, the Turn may be used on a Note, that sinks a Semitone below two Notes on the same Line or Space. always beginning with the first; and also at the End of a Strain, when the last Note is grac'd, as in the following Examples

Some Directions for Singing.

1. In learning the 8 Notes, get the Assistance of some Person, well acquainted with the Tones & Semitones.

2. Chuse that Part, which you can sing with the greatest Ease, and make yourself Master of that first.

3. Sound all high Notes as soft as possible, but low ones hard and full.

4. Pitch your Tune so that the highest and lowest Notes may be sounded distinctly.

The eight Notes Ascending & Descending.

sol.la.mi.fa.sol.la.fa.sol.sol.fa.la.sol.fa.mi.la.sol.s.s. l.l.m.m.f.f. s.s. l.l.f.f.s.s. s.s. f.f. l.l.s.s. f.f.m.m.l.l.s.s.

Thirds, ascending   and descending.

Mear Tune

2.

Canterbury Tune

Windsor Tune

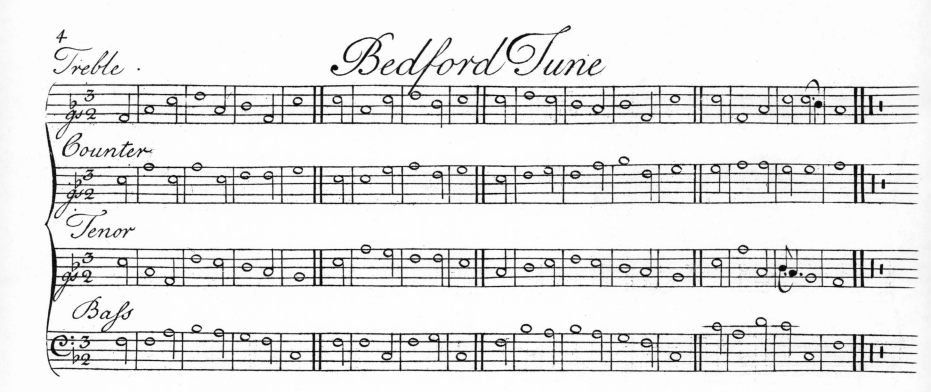

St. Ann's Tune

6

Standish Tune

Crowle Tune

St Davids Tune

8 Treble

Counter

Tenor

Bass

Gloucester Tune

Coleshill Tune

Walsal Tune

St Michael's Tune

Isle of Wight

London New Tune

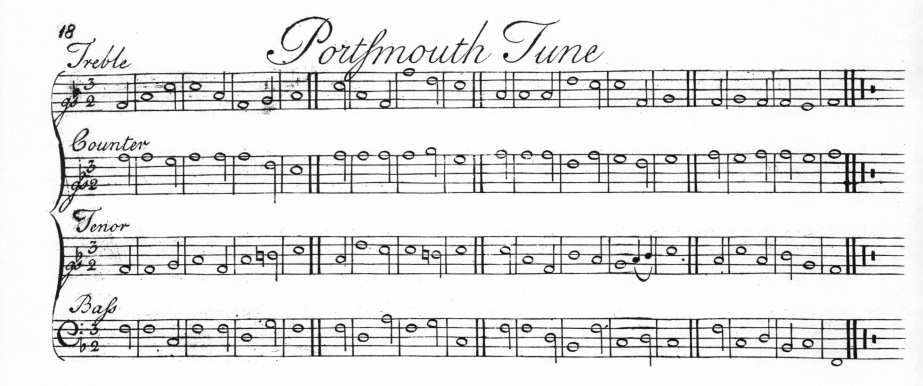

Brunswick Tune.

Cookfield Tune.

Darking. Chorus,

Tenor Solo · Treble · Bass Solo · Counter. · Treble Solo · Tenor · Counter Solo · Bass

St Matthew's Tune,

Rygate Tune.

Treble

Counter

Tenor

Bass

Wirksworth Tune.

Orange Tune,

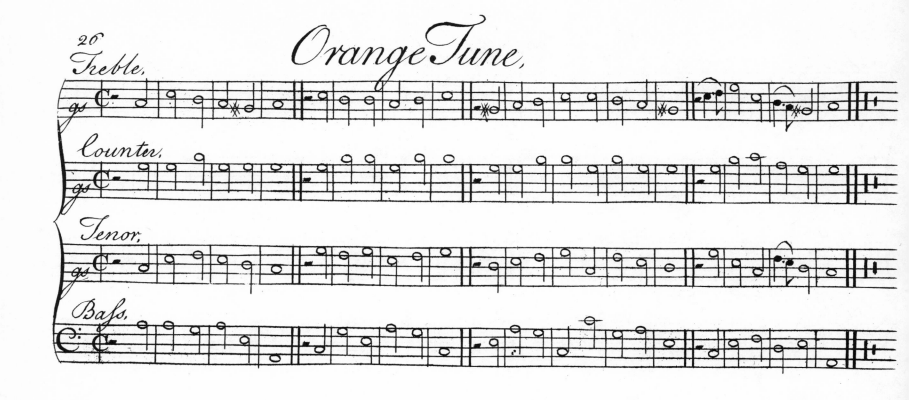

Newcastle Tune.

Southwell Tune.

Derby Tune.

St: Peters Tune.

Bath Tune

The Morning Hymn.

Wells Tune

Willington Tune.

Dagenham

Chorus

The Angels Hymn,

36

Treble

Counter

Tenor

Bass

Leatherhead.

Cranley Tune

Cranley, Continued

The IV Psalm Tune

40

IV *Continued*

The v Psalm Tune

Continued

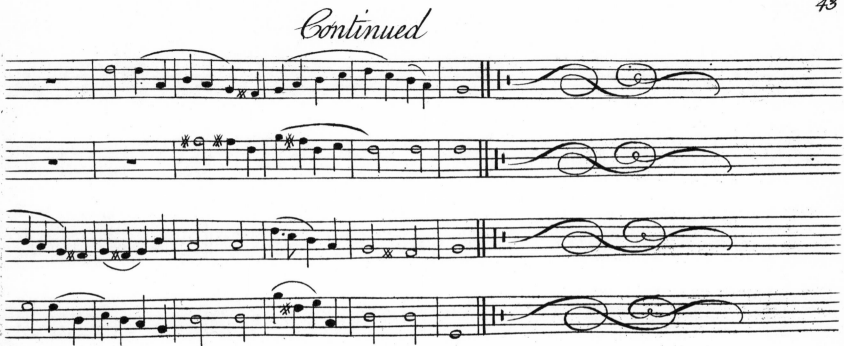

The 8.th Psalm Tune

The 9th Psalm

The 12th Psalm Tune

Continued

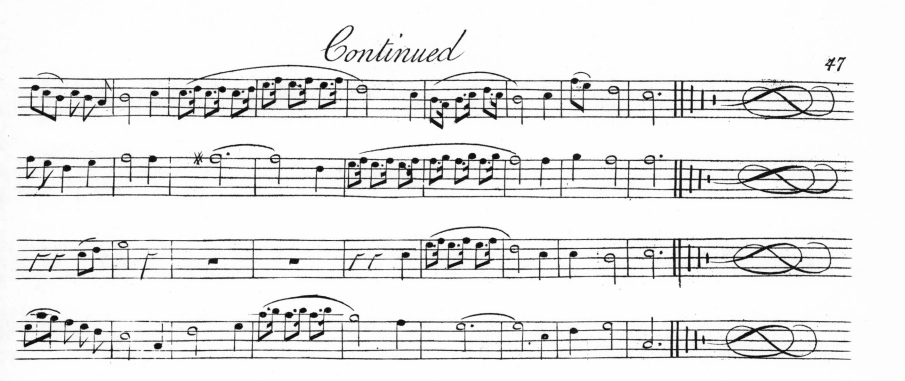

The 15th Psalm Tune

Continued

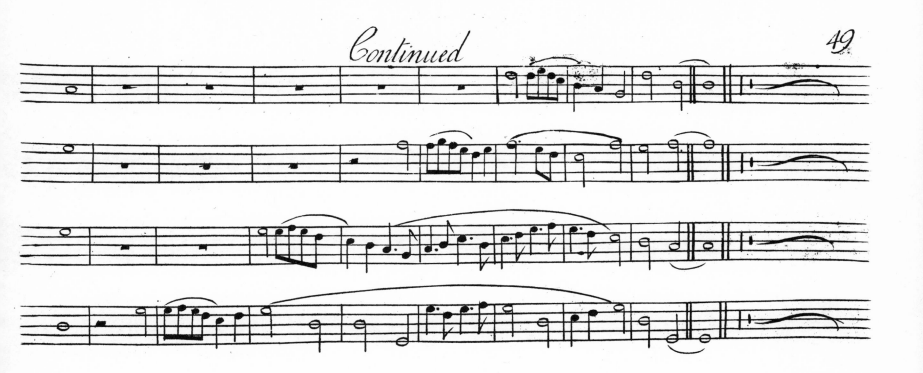

The 23.ᵈ Psalm Tune

50
Treble

Counter

Tenor

Bass

Continued

The 33.d Psalm Tune

Continued

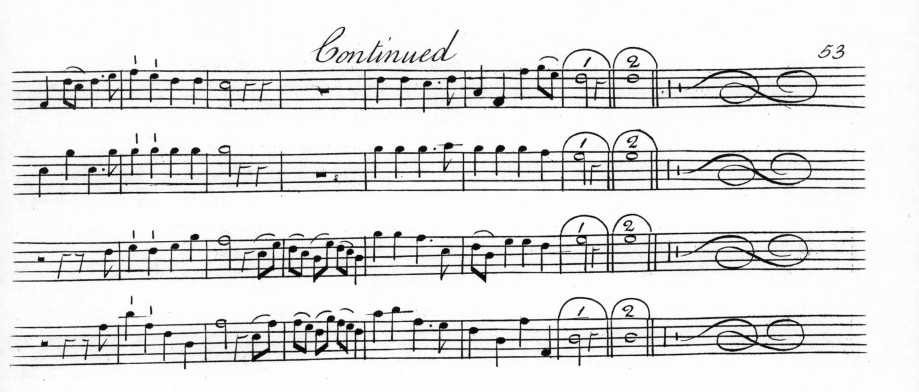

The 40.th Psalm Tune

The 43.ᵈ Psalm Tune

The Old 50.th Psalm Tune

Continued

The New 50th Psalm Tune

Continued

60

The 56th Psalm Tune

The 57.th Psalm Tune

62

The 90.th Psalm Tune

Treble

Counter

Tenor

Bass

* The 95th Psalm Tune

64

The 98.th Psalm Tune

The Old 100 Psalm Tune

65

Treble

Counter

Tenor

Bass

The 102 Psalm Tune

The 112.th Psalm Tune

68 Treble

Counter

Tenor

Bass

Continued

The Old 113.th Psalm Tune

Continued

Continued

The Old 119.th Psalm Tune

Continued

76 Treble

The New 119th Psalm Tune

Continued

The 122.ᵈ Psalm Tune

Continued

The 136.th Psalm Tune

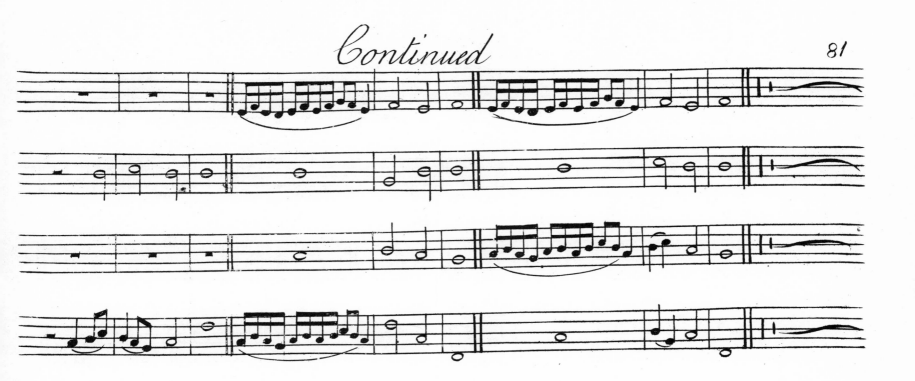

The 145.th Psalm Tune

The 148.ᵗʰ Psalm Tune

The Old 148th Psalm Tune

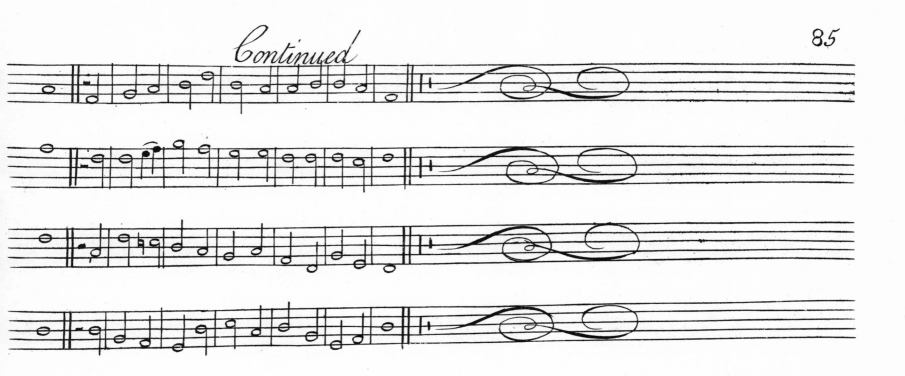

Continued

86

The 149th Psalm Tune

Continued

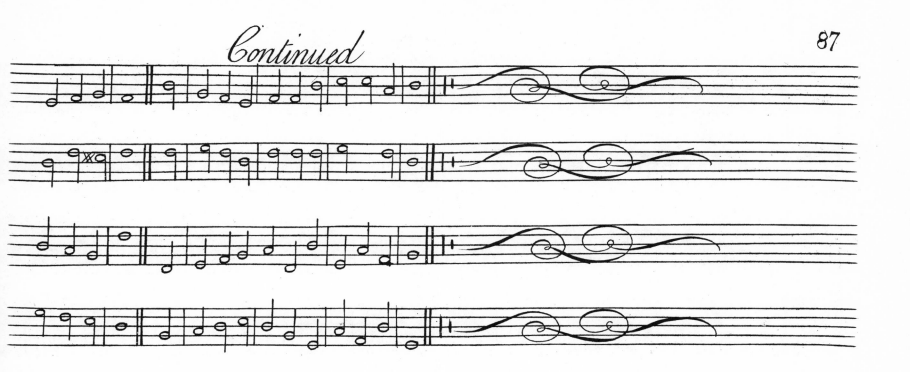

The 150th Psalm Tune

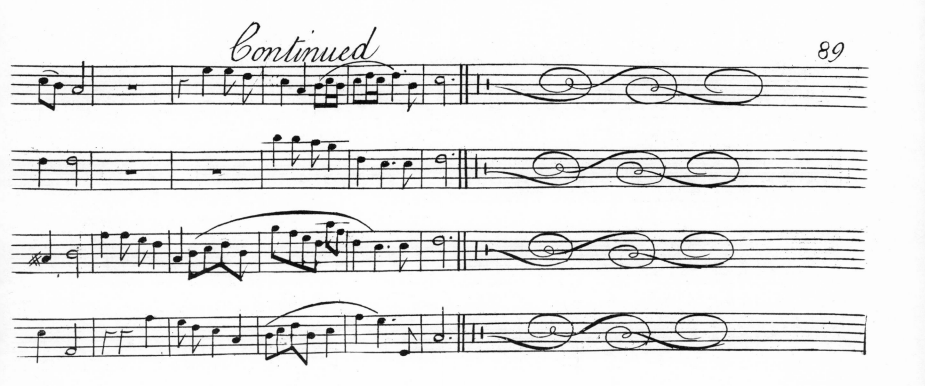

Continued

An Anthem taken out of the 16th Psalm

Treble

Preserve me, O God, preserve me, O God, for in thee have I put my trust: I will thank thee, O God, I will thank

Counter

I will thank thee, O God.

Tenor

Preserve me, O God, preserve me, O God, for in thee have I put my trust. I will thank thee, O God, I will thank

Bass

I will thank thee, O God.

Continued

thee, O God, for giving me warning. My reins also chasten me in the night season, wherefore my heart, where

O God, &c.   wherefore my

thee, O God, for giving me warning. My reins also chasten me in the night season, wherefore my heart, where

O God, &c.   wherefore my

Continued

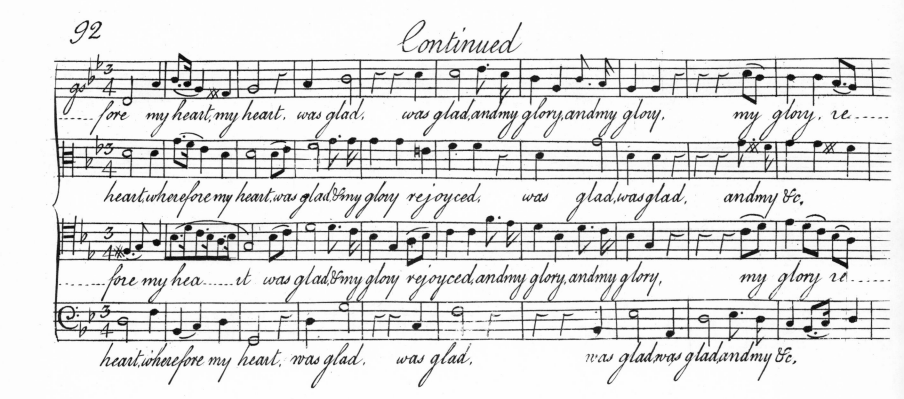

......fore my heart, my heart. was glad.　was glad, and my glory, and my glory,　my glory. re......

heart, wherefore my heart, was glad & my glory rejoyced.　was　glad, was glad,　and my &c.

......fore my hea......rt was glad & my glory rejoyced, and my glory, and my glory,　my glory re......

heart, wherefore my heart. was glad.　was glad,　was glad, was glad, and my &c.

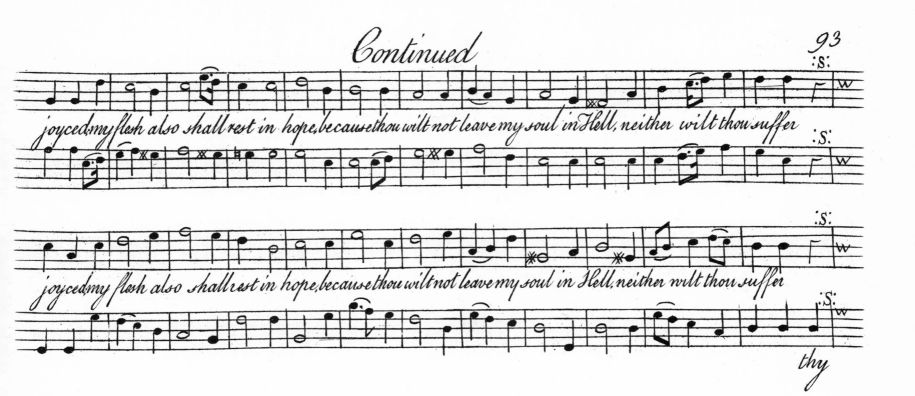

joyced my flesh also shall rest in hope, because thou wilt not leave my soul in Hell, neither wilt thou suffer

joyced my flesh also shall rest in hope, because thou wilt not leave my soul in Hell, neither wilt thou suffer

thy

Continued

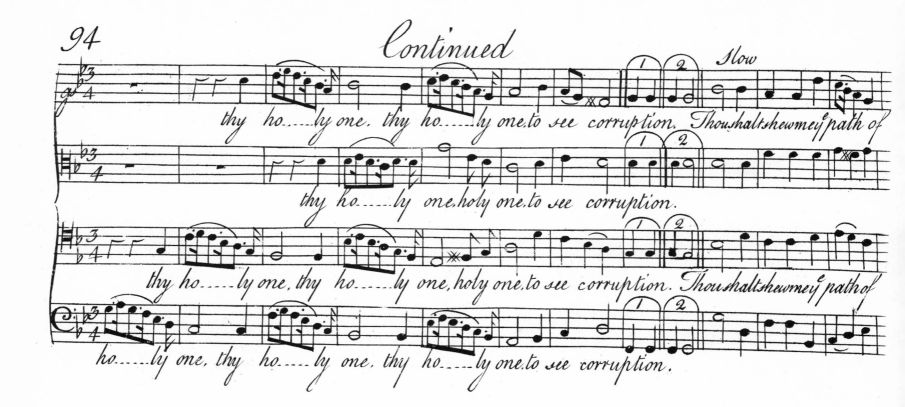

life, in thy presence is fulness, is fullness, is fullness, of joy: and at thy right hand there is pleasure for ever, for

life, in thy presence is fullness, is fullness, of joy: and at thy right hand, there is pleasure for

life, in thy presence is fullness, is fullness, of joy: and at thy right hand, there is pleasure for ever, for

life, in thy presence is fullness, is fullness, is fullness, of joy: and at thy right hand, there is pleasure for

Continued

ever, there is pleasure for. ever, for e...ver more.

ever. is pleasure for ever, for ever more.

ever. for ever, there is pleasure for e....ver more.

ever, there is pleasure. is pleasure, for e..ver more.

An Anthem taken out of the 34.th Psalm

Continued

Treble

continually be in my Mouth. My soul shall make her boast of the Lord: the humble men shall hear thereof, and be glad.

Counter

Tenor

continually be in my mouth. My soul shall make her boast of the Lord: the humble men shall hear thereof, and be glad.

Bass

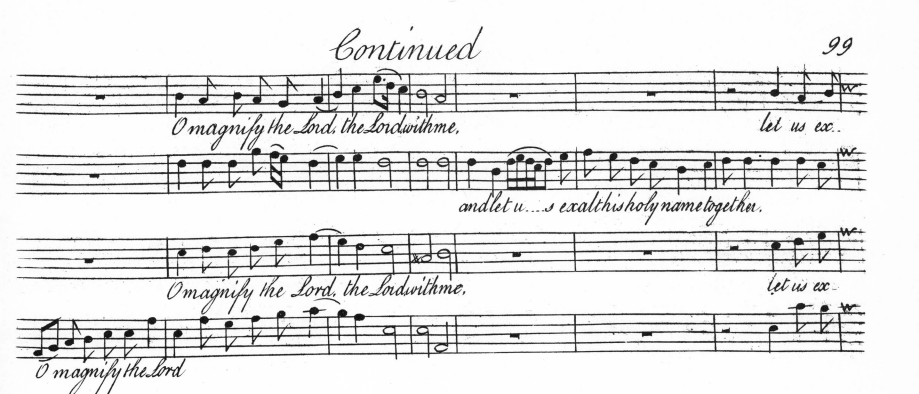

Continued

Treble:

alt his holy Name together. I sought the Lord. and he heard me, he heard me, & deliver'd & deliver'd me from all my fears.

Counter

I sought the Lord & he heard me &c.

Tenor

alt his holy Name together.   I sought the Lord & he heard me. & deliver'd. and deliver'd me. from all my fears.

I sought the Lord & he heard me, he heard me.

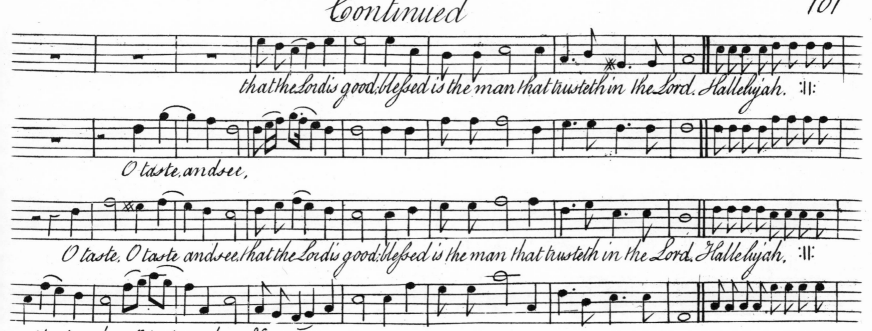

that the Lord is good: blessed is the man that trusteth in the Lord. Hallelujah. :||:

O taste, and see,

O taste, O taste and see, that the Lord is good: blessed is the man that trusteth in the Lord. Hallelujah. :||:

O taste and see, O taste and see, &c.

Continued

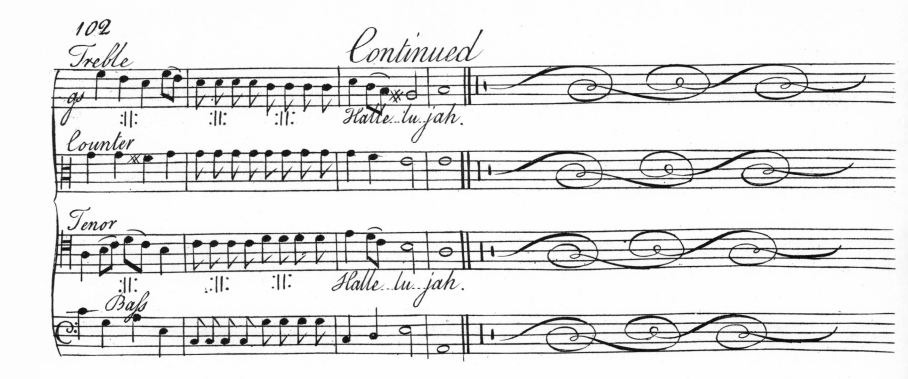

An Anthem taken out of the 100th Psalm

Continued

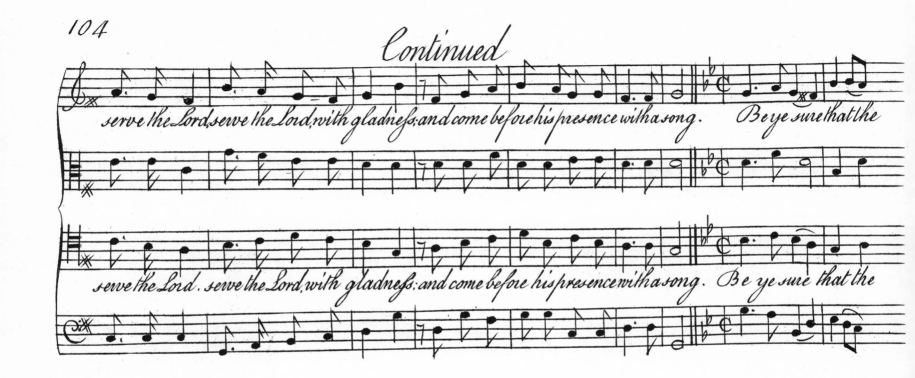

serve the Lord, serve the Lord, with gladness: and come before his presence with a song.   Be ye sure that the

serve the Lord. serve the Lord, with gladness: and come before his presence with a song.   Be ye sure that the

Lord he is God; it is he that hath made us and not we ourselves: we are his people and the sheep of his pasture. ture.

Lord he is God; it's he that hath made us and not we our selves: we are his people and the sheep of his pasture. - ture.

Continued

O go your way into his gates with thanksgiving, and into his cou.........rts

O go your way. &c.

O go your way your way. go you way. in...to his gates with thanksgiving, and into his cou.........rts

O go your way O &c.

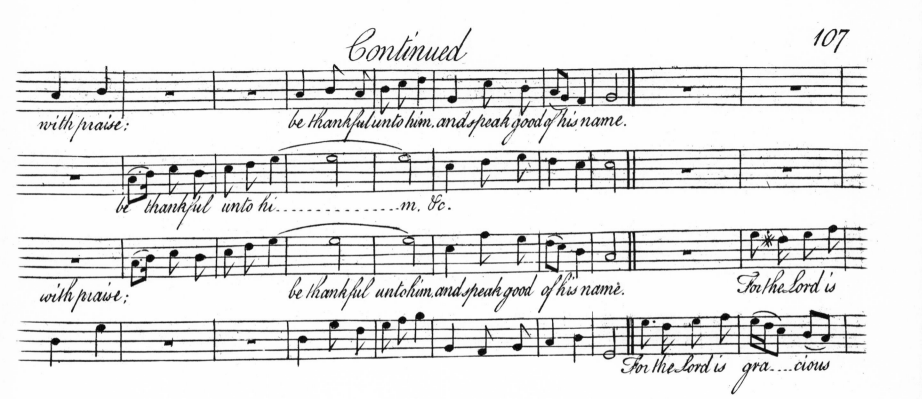

with praise: be thankful unto him, and speak good of his name.

be thankful unto hi................m, &c.

with praise: be thankful unto him, and speak good of his name.   For the Lord is

For the Lord is gra....cious

Continued

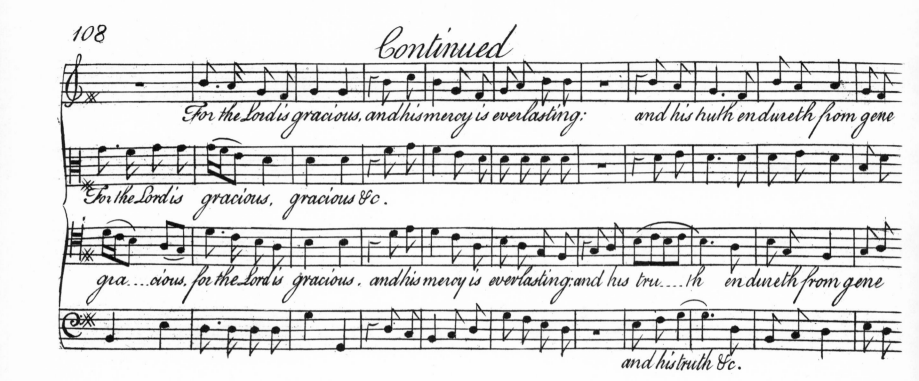

For the Lord is gracious, and his mercy is everlasting: and his truth endureth from gene

For the Lord is   gracious,   gracious &c.

gra....cious, for the Lord is gracious, and his mercy is everlasting; and his tru.....th   endureth from gene

and his truth &c.

Bass Solus

ration t......o generation. Gl........ory be to the Father, As it was in the beginning.

Tenr Solus

Gl........ory be to the Son.

Counter & Bass

ration t......o generation. Gl........ory be to the holy Ghost, As it was in the beginning. is

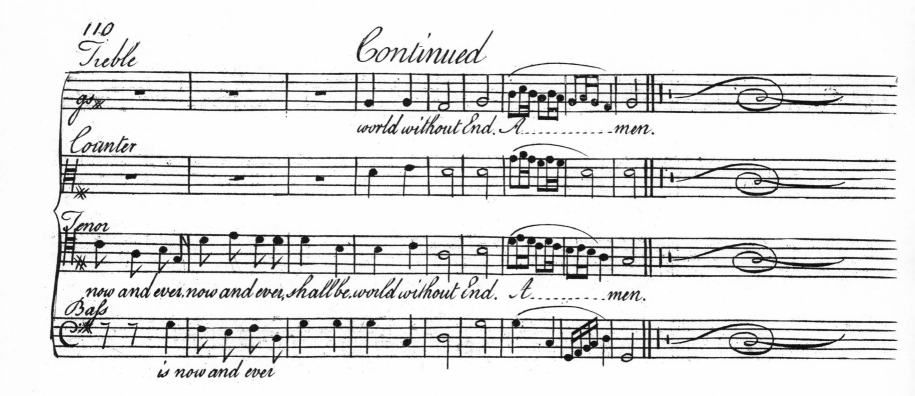

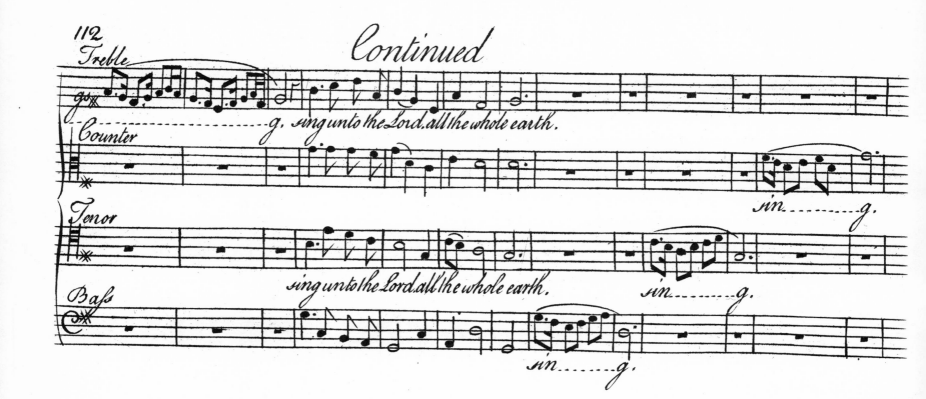

Continued

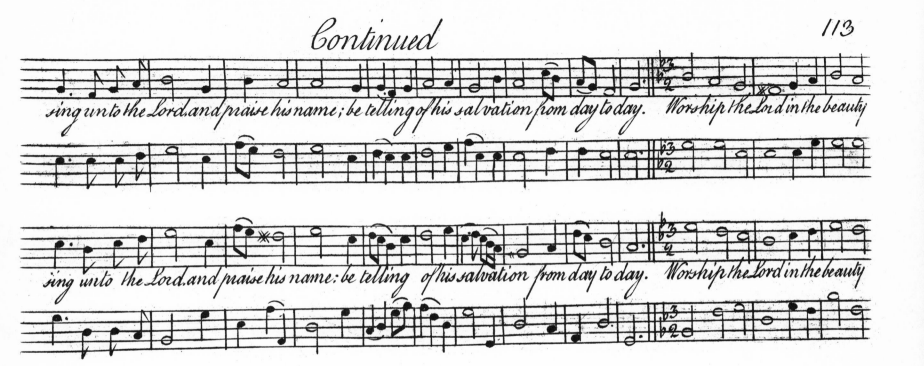

sing unto the Lord, and praise his name; be telling of his salvation from day to day. Worship the Lord in the beauty

sing unto the Lord, and praise his name: be telling of his salvation from day to day. Worship the Lord in the beauty

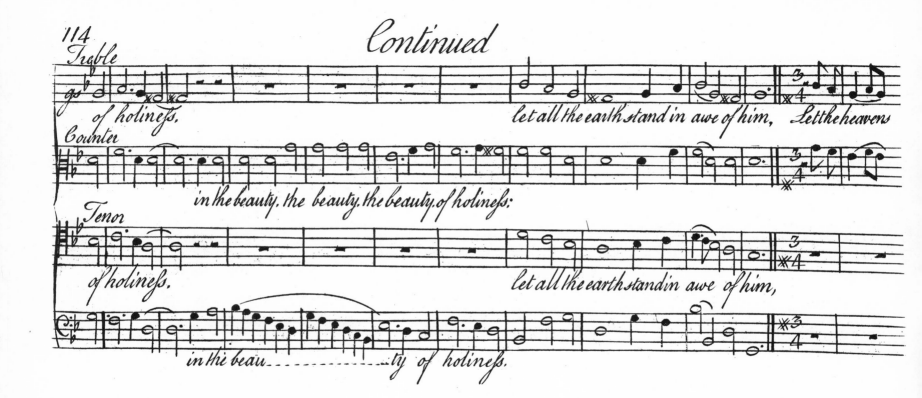

Continued

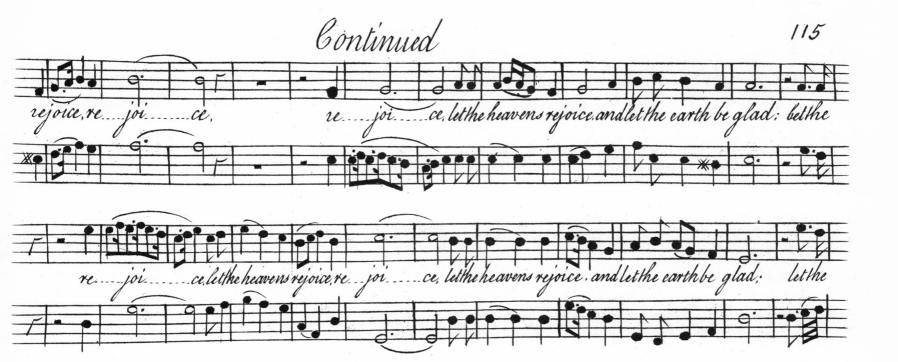

rejoice, re....joi.........ce,   re.....joi.........ce, let the heavens rejoice, and let the earth be glad: be the

re......joi.........ce, let the heavens rejoice, re....joi.........ce, let the heavens rejoice. and let the earth be glad;   let the

Continued

Sea make a noise, and all that therein is; let the field be joyful, and all that is in it. Then shall the trees re

Sea make a noise, and all that therein is: let the field be joyful, and all that is in it. Then shall the trees re

Continued

joice, rejoice, re.......joi....ce, before the Lord. Hallelujah, Hallelujah, Hallelujah, Hallelujah, Hallelujah, Hallelujah.

......joi...........ce, before the Lord. Hallelujah, Hallelujah, Hallelujah. Ha.............lelujah.

.....oice, rejoice, rejoi......ce.   Hallelujah, Hallelujah, Hallelujah;

Continued

with the voice of melody, with the voice the voice. the voice, the voice, the voice of melody:

singing to God with the voice of melody, with the voi........ce, the voice of melody: for the

God with the voice. the voice, of melody, with the voice, the voice. the voi......ce. the &c.

Continued

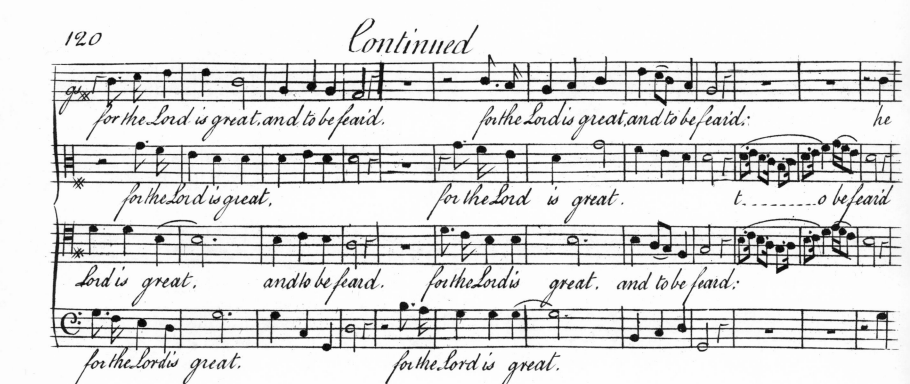

for the Lord is great, and to be feaird.   for the Lord is great, and to be feaird: he

for the Lord is great,   for the Lord is great.   t..........o be feaird

Lord is great.   and to be feard.   for the Lord is   great.   and to be feaird:

for the Lord is great.   for the Lord is great.

Continued

is the great king upon all the earth.

upon all the earth. God is gone up with a

he is the great king upon

upon all the earth, upon al............l the earth.

is the great king

upon al.........l upon all the earth.

Continued

merry noise,

and the Lord with the

and the Lord with the sound of the trumpet, of the tru............mpet, and the Lord with the

of the tru............mpet

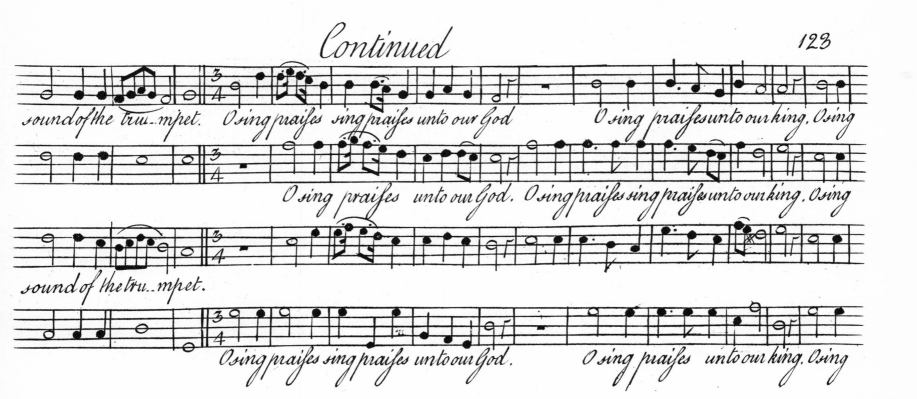

sound of the tru..mpet.   O sing praises sing praises unto our God   O sing praises unto our king. O sing

O sing praises   unto our God. O sing praises sing praise unto our king. O sing

sound of the tru..mpet.

O sing praises sing praises unto our God.   O sing praises   unto our king. O sing

Continued

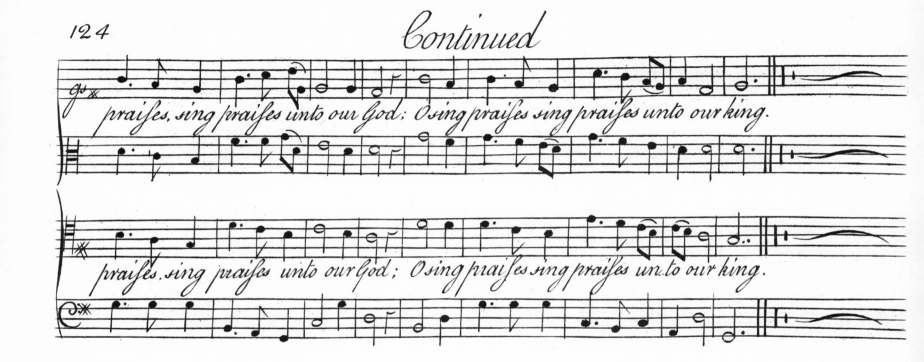

praises, sing praises unto our God; O sing praises sing praises unto our king.

praises, sing praises unto our God; O sing praises sing praises unto our king.

Continued

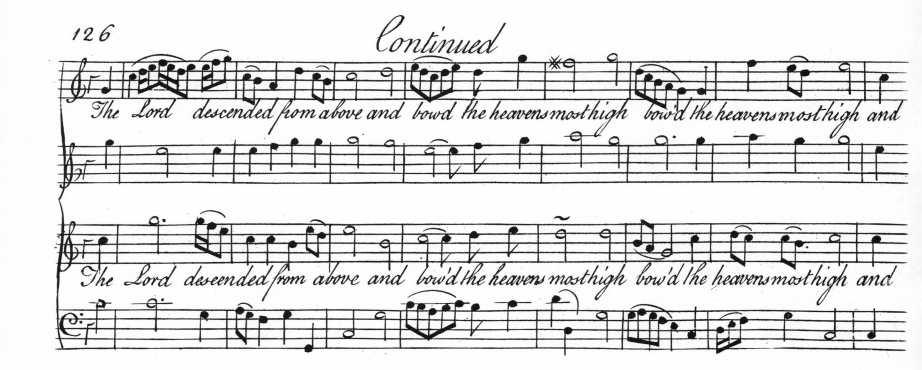

The Lord descended from above and bow'd the heavens most high bow'd the heavens most high and

The Lord descended from above and bow'd the heavens most high bow'd the heavens most high and

underneath his feet, he cast the darkness, the darkness of the sky. On cherubs & on cherubims full royal.

underneath his feet, he cast the darkness, the darkness of the sky. On cherubs & on cherubims full royal.

Continued

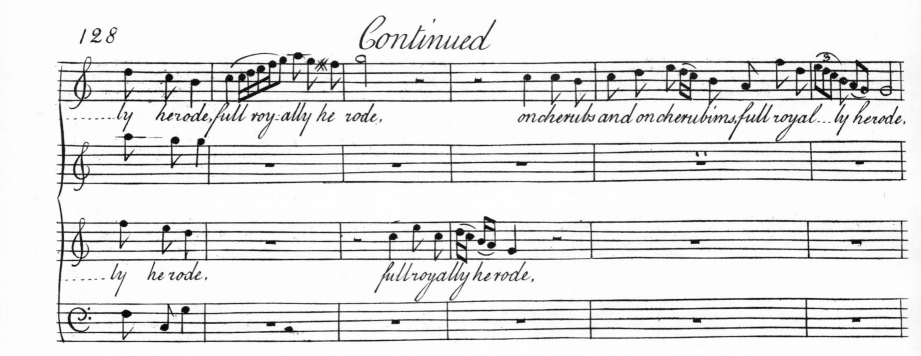

...... ly   he rode, full roy-ally he rode.   on cherubs and on cherubims, full royal ... ly he rode.

...... ly   he rode.   full royally he rode,

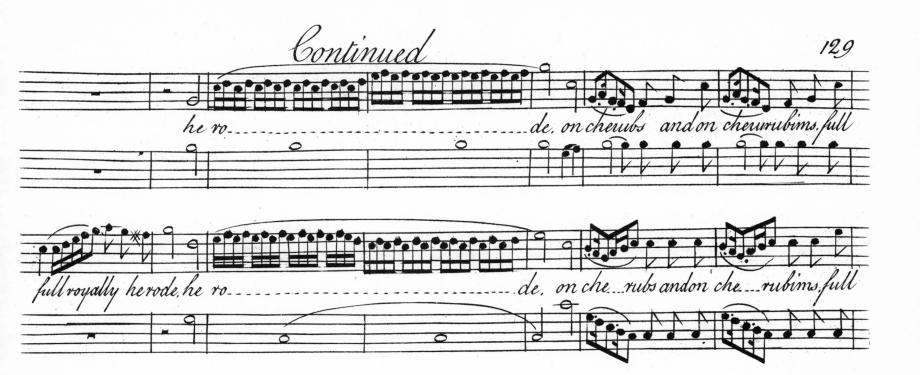

Continued

he ro..de, on cherubs and on cherrubims, full

full royally he rode, he ro...de, on che....rubs and on che....rubims, full

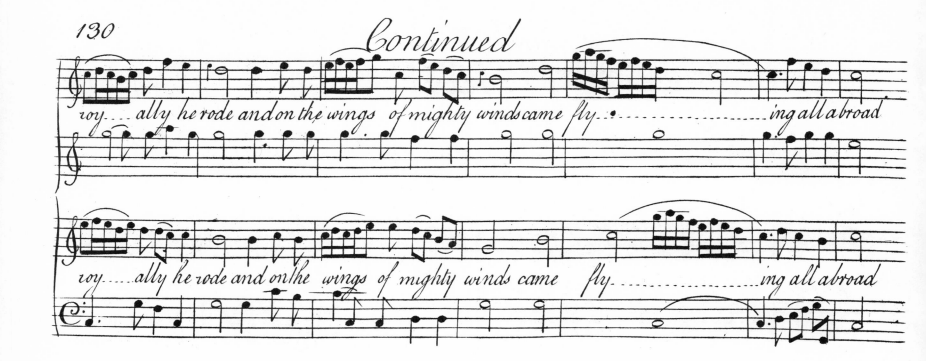

Continued

roy.....ally he rode and on the wings of mighty winds came fly.................ing all abroad

roy.....ally he rode and on the wings of mighty winds came fly.................ing all abroad

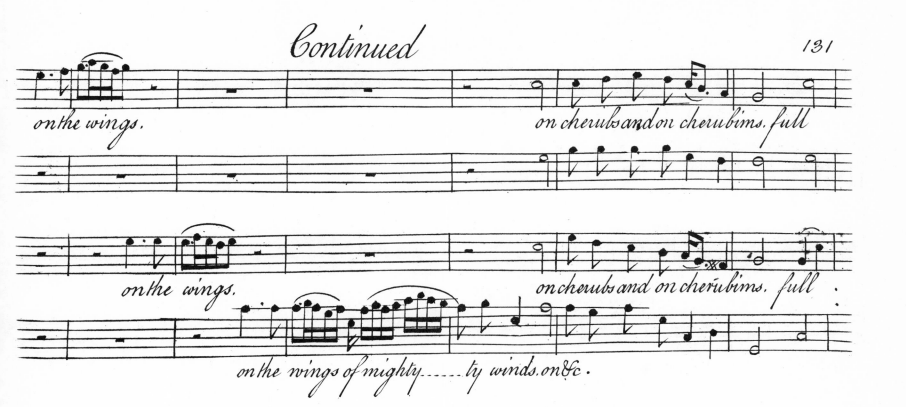

on the wings.   on cherubs and on cherubims. full

on the wings.   on cherubs and on cherubims. full.

on the wings of mighty.......ty winds. on &c.

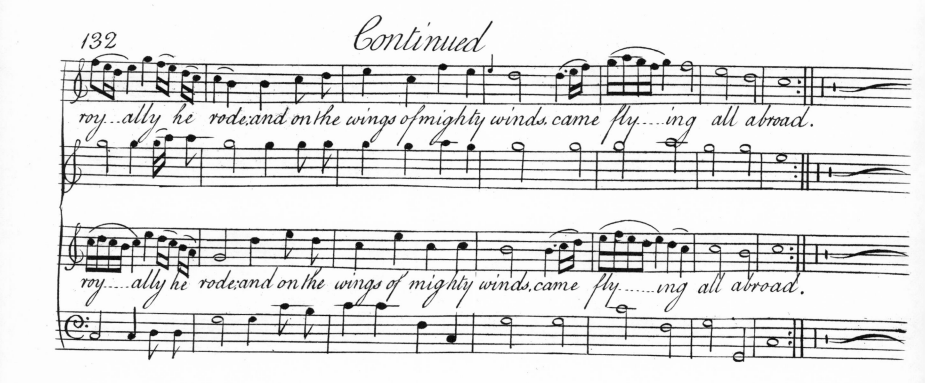

1st Treble *An Anthem* taken out of the 97 *Psalm*

Jehovah reigns, let all the earth, let all the earth, all, all, the earth, rejoice, all, let all the earth, in his just govern-
d. Let all the isles with sacred mirth, with sacred mirth, let all the isles rejoice, all, with sacred mirth, in his applause u-

2. Treble

Jehovah reigns, let all the earth, let all the earth, all, all. &c.

Tenor

Jehovah reigns, let all the earth, all the earth, let all the earth rejoice, all, let all the earth, in his just gov-
Let all the isles with sacred mirth, sacred mirth, let all the isles rejoice, all, with sacred mirth, in his ap-plause

Continued

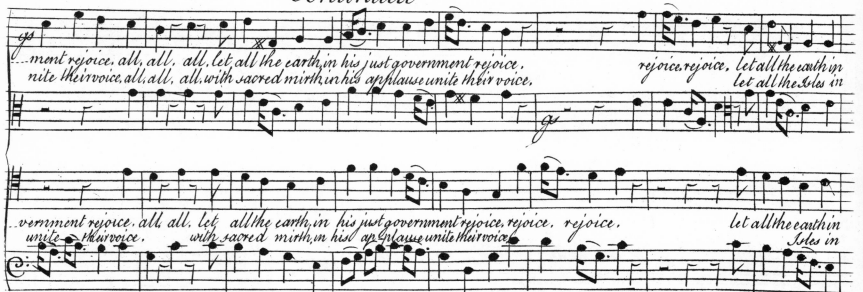

...ment rejoice, all, all, all, let all the earth, in his just government rejoice.
...nite their voice, all, all, all, with sacred mirth, in his applause unite their voice.
rejoice, rejoice, let all the earth in
let all the Isles in

...vernment rejoice, all, all, let all the earth, in his just government rejoice, rejoice, rejoice.
...unite their voice.
with sacred mirth, in his applause unite their voice.
let all the earth in
Isles in

his just government rejoice.
his applause unite their voice.

his dazling glory shroud in state.

his just government rejoice.
his applause unite their voice.

Darkness and clouds, of awful shade, his dazling glory shroud in state.

Continued

Justice and truth his guards are made, and fix'd by his pavilion wait.

Treble & Bass brisk

Devouring fire before his face, de......

Devouring fire. before his face, be......

Justice and truth his guards are made, and fix'd by his pavilion wait.

vouring fire his foes around with vengeance struck,

fore his face his &c.

His lightning set the world on blaze earth saw it and with terror shook   The proudest hills his

His lightning set the world on blaze earth saw it and with terror shook   presence felt, their

Continued

hight nor strength could help afford. The proudest hills like wax did melt in presence of th'almighty Lord.

Slow

The heav'ns his righteousness to shew, with storms of fire, his foes pursu'd: and all the trembling world be

Tenor & Bass · 1st & 2 Trebles

low have his descending glory view'd. Glad sion of thy triumph heard, and Judahs daughters were o're joyd.

Treble & Bass

because thy righteous judgements Lord, have pagan pride and power destroy'd.

Continued

Rejoice, ye righteous, in the Lord, memorials of his holiness, deep in your faithful breasts record;

Rejoice, ye righteous, in the Lord, memorials of his holiness deep in your faithful breasts record;

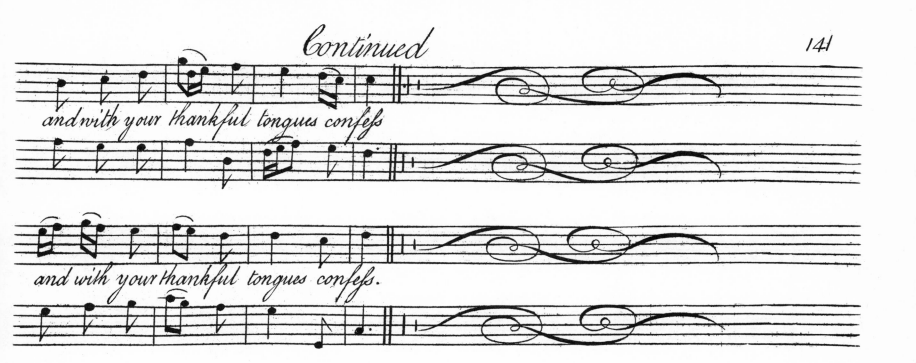

Continued

Continued

great is ý Lord, & marvellous. There is no end, there is no end, there is no end, no end, of his greatness.

great is ý Lord, & marvellous. There is no end, there is no end, there is no end, no end, of his greatness.

146

Continued

marvellous acts.

And I will also tell, also tell, of thy greatness.

And I will also tell, and I will also tell, of thy greatness.

marvellous acts.

And I will also tell, and I will also tell, also tell, of thy greatness.

and I will also tell, and I will also tell, and I will also tell, of thy greatness.

Continued

And let all flesh give thanks, & let all flesh give thanks, & let all flesh give thanks, unto his holy.

And let all flesh give thanks, & let all flesh give thanks, & let all flesh give thanks. unto his holy

Continued

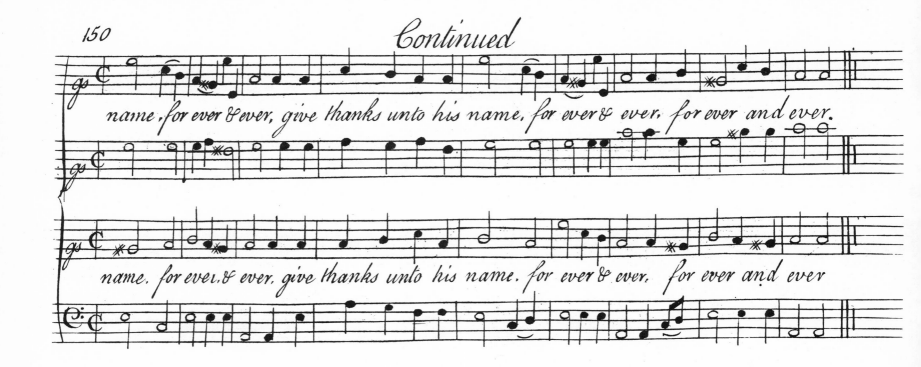

name, for ever & ever, give thanks unto his name, for ever & ever, for ever and ever.

name, for ever & ever, give thanks unto his name, for ever & ever, for ever and ever

Continued

wondrous works. Rejoice in his ho....ly name, let y̌ heart of them of them rejoice, that see........k y̌ Lord. Seek y̌

Rejoice in his holy name, let y̌ heart of them rejoice, &c.

Lord, seek y̌ᵉ Lord, & his, & his strength, See........................k his face e...ver more.

Seek y̌ Lord, seek y̌ᵉ Lord, & his strength, &c.

Chorus   **Continued**

Hallelujah, hallelujah, hallelujah, let us sing hallelujah to our God, hallelujah to our King.

Hallelujah, hallelujah, hallelujah, let us sing, hallelujah to our God, hallelujah to our King.

Continued

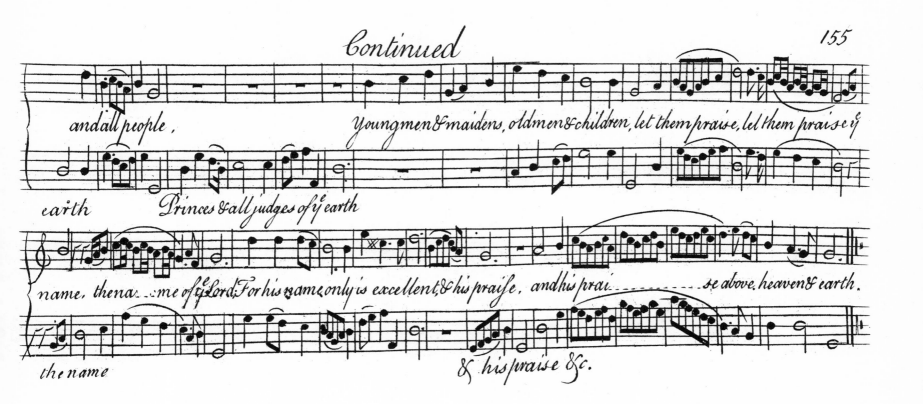

and all people.　　　　　　Young men & maidens, old men & children, let them praise, let them praise y^e

earth　　　　Princes & all judges of y^e earth

name. the na......me of y^e Lord. For his name only is excellent, & his praise, and his prai............se above. heaven & earth.

the name　　　　　　　& his praise &c.

156 An Anthem taken from the 7:th Chapter of Job

Is there not an appointed time to man upon earth, are not his days also as the days of an hireling?

Is there not an appointed time to man upon earth, are not his days also as the days of an hireling.

Treble solo

I'm made to possess

and wearisome nights are appointed to me. When I lie down,

months of vanity.

And wearisome nights &c.

when I

and wearisome nights

and wearisome nights are appointed to me.

are appointed to me.

Continued

I say, when shall I arise, & the night be gone?

lie down.

when I lie down.   I say, when shall I arise, & the night be gone?   I'm full of

when I lie down, when I lie down, &c.   I'm full of tosing too & fro.

unto the dawning of the day.

tosing

My flesh is cloth'd with worms. My skin is

tosing to & fro, unto the dawning of y[e] day.

tosing &c.

My flesh is cloth'd with worms, and clods of dust; My skin is

Continued

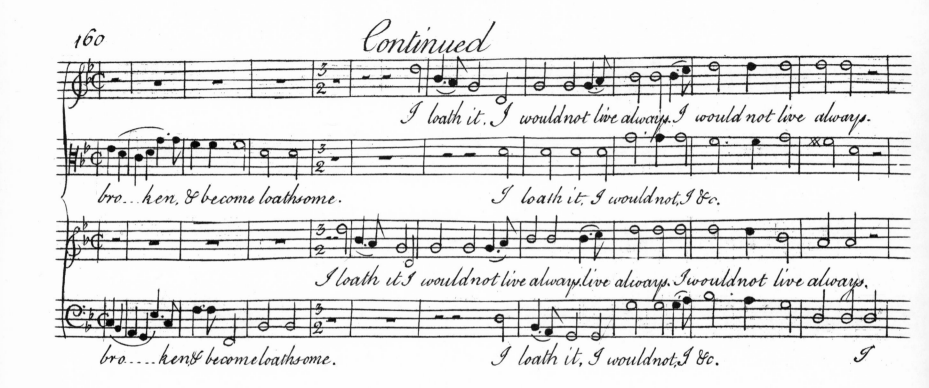

I loath it. I would not live always. I would not live always.

bro...ken, & become loathsome.   I loath it, I would not, I &c.

I loath it I would not live always. live always. I would not live always.

bro.....ken & become loathsome.   I loath it, I would not, I &c.   I

I wouldnot live always.

I loath it, I wouldnot live always. Let me alone, for my days are vanity . my days are vanity.

loath it, I wou'd not, I &c.

Continued

Tenor Solo

My days are swifter

than a weavers

shuttle. & are spent

with......out hope.

O remember that my life. my life. is wind: mine eyes shall no more see good.

O remember y my life. is wind &c.

O remember that my life. my life. is wind: mine eyes shall no more see good.

Continued

As the cloud is consumed & vanisheth away, so he, that goeth down to the grave, shall come up no more; for now

As y cloud is consumed, and vanisheth away, so &c.

more

As the cloud is consumed & vanisheth away. so he, that goeth down to the grave; shall come up no more; for now

more

As y cloud is consumed & vanisheth away, so &c.

An Anthem taken from the 150.th Psalm

Let the shrill tru........mpets warlike voice, make rocks & hills his praise rebound;

Let the shrill trumpets warlike voice, warlike voice, make rocks & hills his praise rebound;

warlike, warlike, voice &c.

Continued
Adagio

...make rock's & hills his praise rebound. Praise him with ha............rps   melodious noise,

make rocks & hills his praise rebound. Praise him with harps melodious noise, melodious noise,

Continued

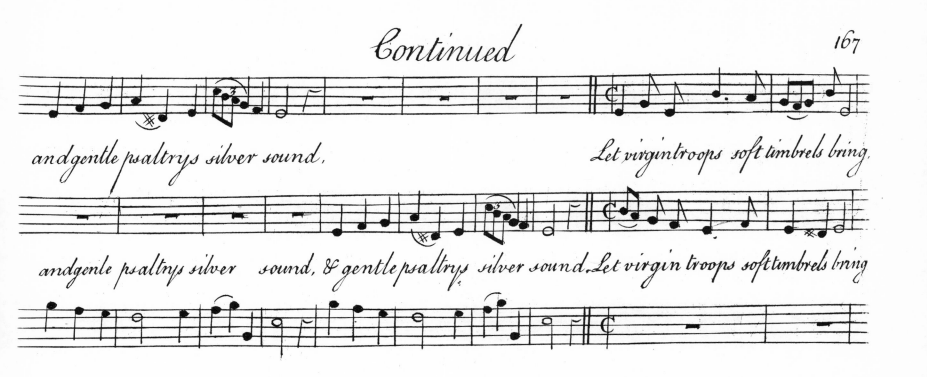

and gentle psaltrys silver sound,   Let virgin troops soft timbrels bring,

and gentle psaltrys silver   sound, & gentle psaltrys silver sound. Let virgin troops soft timbrels bring

Continued

and some with graceful motion dance,   Let instruments of various

and some with graceful motion dance. Let instruments of various

Continued

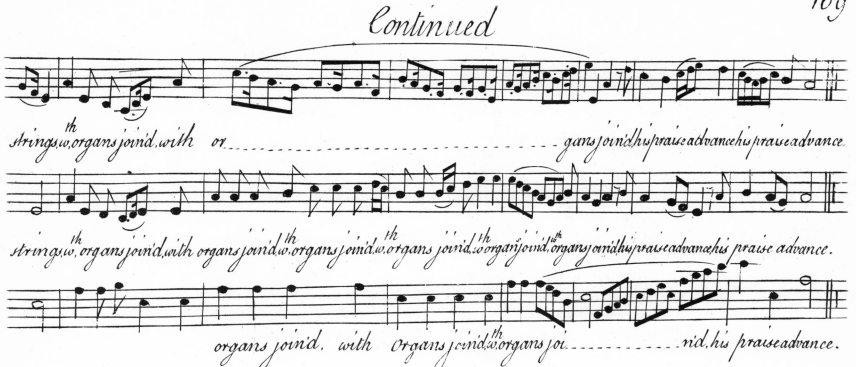

St Mathew's

To heaven I lift my waiting eyes, there all my hopes are laid the Lord that built y⁰ earth & skyes is my perpetual aid

There all my hopes are laid, the Lord that built y⁰ earth & skyes, is my perpetual aid.

3
He will sustain our feeble powers,
With his Almighty arm,
And watch our most unguarded hours,
Against invading harm.

4
Israel rejoice and rest secure.
Thy keeper is the Lord;
His wakefull eyes employ his pow'r,
For thine eternal guard.

Their feet shall never slide or fall, Whom he designs to keep; His ear attends the softest call, His eyes can never Sleep.

Their feet shall never slide or fall, whom he designs to keep; His ear attends the softest call, His eyes can never sleep.

5

Nor scorching sun, nor sickly moon,
Shall have his leave to smite;
He shields thy head from burning noon,
From blasting damps at night.

6

He guards thy soul, he keeps thy breath,
Where thickest dangers come;
Go and return secure from death,
Till God commands thee home.

Palmi's

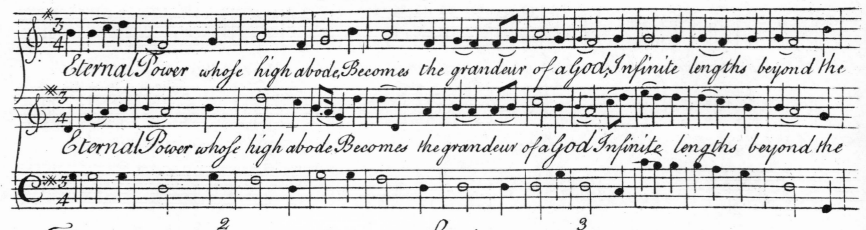

Eternal Power whose high abode, Becomes the grandeur of a God, Infinite lengths beyond the

Eternal Power whose high abode Becomes the grandeur of a God Infinite lengths beyond the

2

Thee while the first archangel sings.
He hides his face behind his wings,
And ranks of shining thrones around,
Fall worshiping and spread the ground.

3

Lord what shall earth and ashes do.
We would adore our maker too,
From sin and dust to thee we cry,
The great, the holy, and the high.

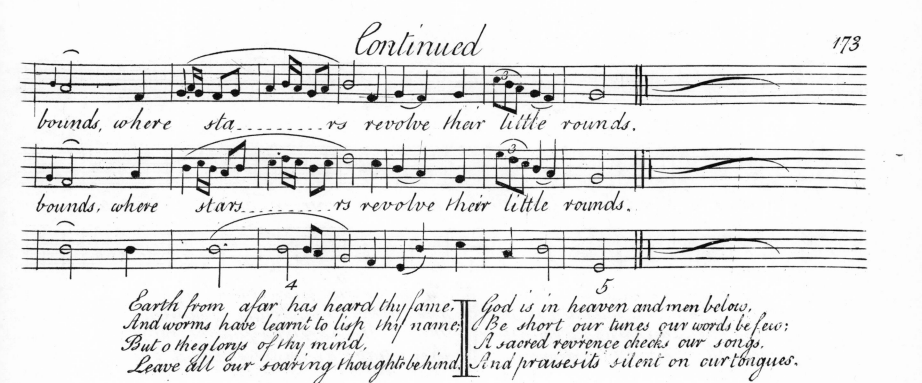

bounds, where sta...........rs revolve their little rounds.

bounds, where stars...........rs revolve their little rounds.

4

Earth from afar has heard thy fame,
And worms have learnt to lisp thy name;
But o the glorys of thy mind,
Leave all our soaring thoughts behind.

5

God is in heaven and men below,
Be short our tunes our words be few;
A sacred rev'rence checks our songs,
And praises its silent on our tongues.

Kettelbys

Praise ye the Lord, tis good to raise, Our hearts and voices in his praise, His nature and his

2
He form'd the stars those heav'nly flames,
He counts their numbers calls their names,
His wisdom's vast, and knows no bounds,
A deep, where all our thoughs are drown'd.

3
Sing to the Lord exalt him high.
Who spreads his clouds around the sky.
There he prepares the fruitful rain,
Nor lets the drops descend in vain.

works invite, To make this duty our delight, To make this duty our delight.

He makes the grass the hills adorn,
And cloths the smiling fields with corn;
The beasts with food his hands supply,
And the young ravens when they cry.

What is the creatures skill or force,
The sprightly man or warlike horse?
The piercing wit, the active limb,
All are too mean delights for him.

Italian

O God, my God, my all thou art, Ere shines the dawn of rising day; Thy sov'reign light with in my heart,

In blessing thee, with grateful songs.
My happy life shall glide away,
The praise, that to thy Name belongs.
Hourly with lifted hands I'll pay.

2

Abundant sweetness while I sing.
Thy love my ravish'd soul o'e flows,
Secure in thee my God and king,
Of glory, that no period knows.

3

Thine all' en live_ _ _ _ _ _ _ _ _ _ Thine all' en liv'ning pow'r display.

Thy name, O Lord, upon my bed,
Dwells on my lips, & fires my thought.
With trembling awe in midnight shade,
I muse on all thine hands have wrought.

In all I do I feel thine aid,
Therefore thy greatness will I sing,
O God, who bidst my heart be glad,
Beneath the shadow of thy wing.

Publick Worship

178

Lo God is here, let us adore; And own how dreadful is this place; Let all within us feel his pow'r.

Lo God is here, him day and night,
Th'united quires of angels sing,
To him, enthron'd above all height,

Heavens host their noblest praises bring,
Disdain not, Lord, our meaner song,
Who praise the with a stamm'ring tongue.

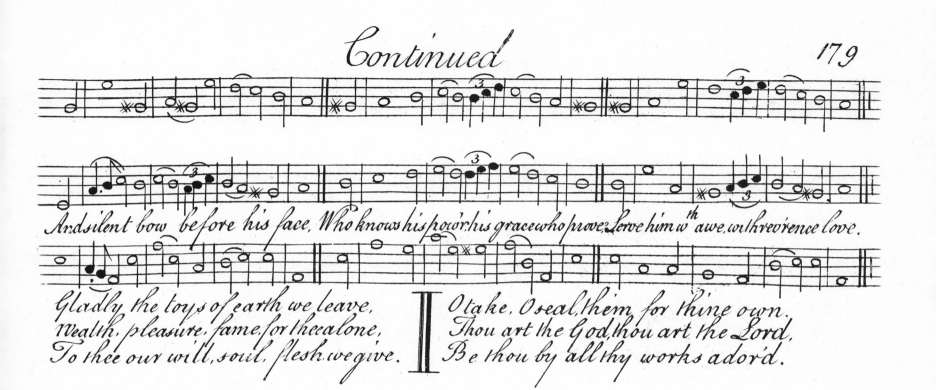

And silent bow before his face, Who knows his pow'r, his grace who proves, Serve him w.th awe, with rev'rence love.

Gladly the toys of earth we leave,
Wealth, pleasure, fame, for thee alone,
To thee our will, soul, flesh we give.

O take, O seal, them for thine own.
Thou art the God, thou art the Lord,
Be thou by all thy works ador'd.

Sky Lark

180

When all thy mercies, O my God, My rising soul surveys, Transported with the view I'm lost In wonder love

To all my weak complaints and cries,
   Thy mercy lent an ear.
E'er yet my feeble thoughts had learn'd,
   To form themselves in prayer.

Unnumber'd comforts to my soul,
   Thy tender care bestow'd.
Before my infant heart conciev'd.
   From whom those comforts flow'd.

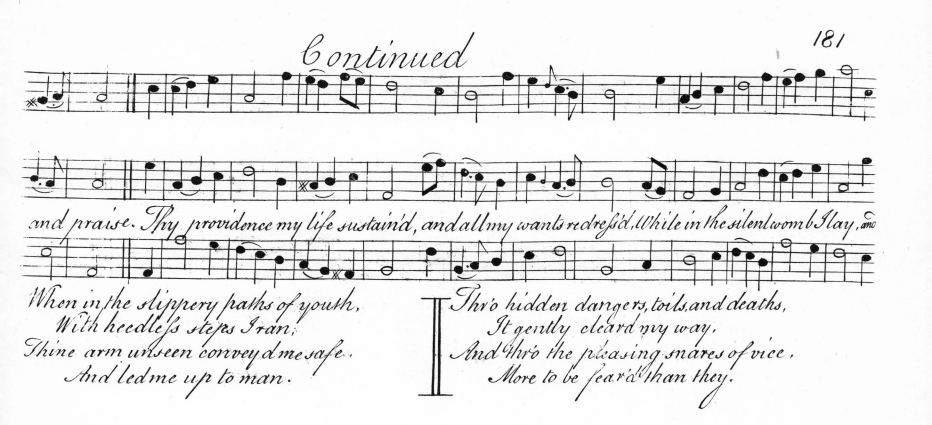

Continued

and praise. Thy providence my life sustain'd, and all my wants redress'd. While in the silent womb I lay, and

When in the slippery paths of youth,
    With heedless steps I ran,
Thine arm unseen convey'd me safe,
    And led me up to man.

Thro' hidden dangers, toils, and deaths,
    It gently clear'd my way,
And thro' the pleasing snares of vice,
    More to be fear'd than they.

Continued

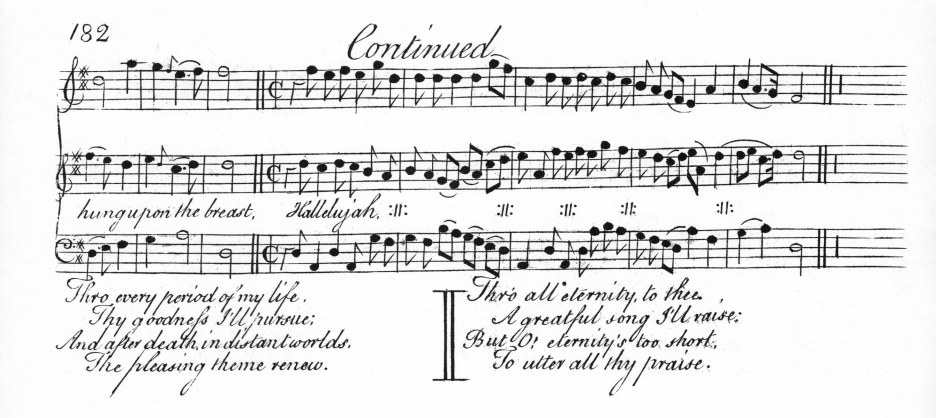

hung upon the breast.   Hallelujah. :||:   :||:   :||:   :||:   :||:   :||:

Thro' every period of my life.
Thy goodness I'll pursue;
And after death, in distant worlds.
The pleasing theme renew.

Thro' all eternity, to thee.
A greatful song I'll raise:
But O! eternity's too short,
To utter all thy praise.

Kettering

The spacious firmament on high. With all the blue ethereal sky. And spangled heav'ns a shining frame

Their great original proclaim. Th'unwearied sun from day to day. Does his creators pow'r display: And publish-

es to ev'ry land, The work of an almighty hand, The work of an almighty hand.

Soon as the evening shades prevail,	What though in solemn silence all,
The moon takes up the wondrous tale,	Move round the dark terrestreal ball,
And nightly to the listning earth,	What tho' nor real voice nor sound,
Repeats the story of her birth;	Amid their radiant orbs be found;
Whilst all the stars, that round her burn,	In reason's ear they all rejoice,
And all the planets, in their turn,	And utter forth a glorious voice,
Confirm the tidings as they rowl,	For ever singing, as they Shine,
And spread the truth from pole to pole.	The hand that made us is divine.

Resurrection

Rejoice, the Lord is king, your Lord and king adore: Mortals give thanks and sing. And triumph evermore.

Jesus the Saviour reigns.
The God of truth and love;
When he had purg'd our stains.
He took his seat above.
Lift up your heart. lift up your voice.
Rejoice. again I say; rejoice.

His kingdom cannot fail.
He rules ore earth and heav'n:
The keys of death and hell
Are to our Jesus given.
Lift up your hearts. lift up your voice.
Rejoice. again I say. rejoice.

Continued

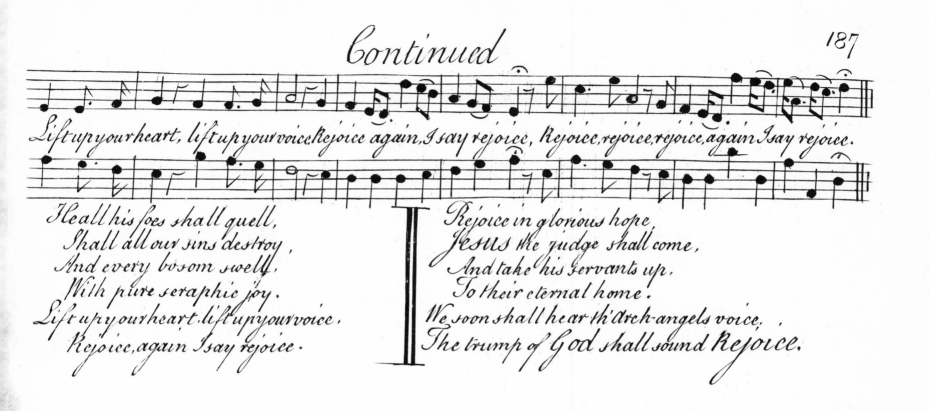

Lift up your heart, lift up your voice Rejoice again, I say rejoice, Rejoice, rejoice, rejoice, again I say rejoice.

He all his foes shall quell,
 Shall all our sins destroy,
And every bosom swell,
 With pure seraphic joy.
Lift up your heart, lift up your voice,
 Rejoice, again I say rejoice.

Rejoice in glorious hope,
 Jesus the judge shall come,
And take his servants up,
 To their eternal home.
We soon shall hear th' Arch-angels voice,
 The trump of God shall sound Rejoice.

Judgment

When the fierce north wind, with his airy forces, Rears up the Baltick to a foaming fury,

How the poor sailors stand amaz'd and tremble,
While the hoarse thunder, like a bloody trumpet,
Roars a loud onset to the gaping waters,
        Quick to devour them.

Such shall the noise be, and the wild disorder,
(If things eternal may be like these earthly)
Such the dire terror. when the great archangel
        Shakes the creation.

Tears the strong pillars of the vault of heaven,
Breaks up old marble. the repose of princes,
See the graves open. and the bones arising,
        Flames all around 'em.

Hark the shrill outcries of the guilty wretches!
Lively bright horror. and amazing anguish,
Stare thro' their eye lids. while the living worm lies
        Gnawing within them.

Continued

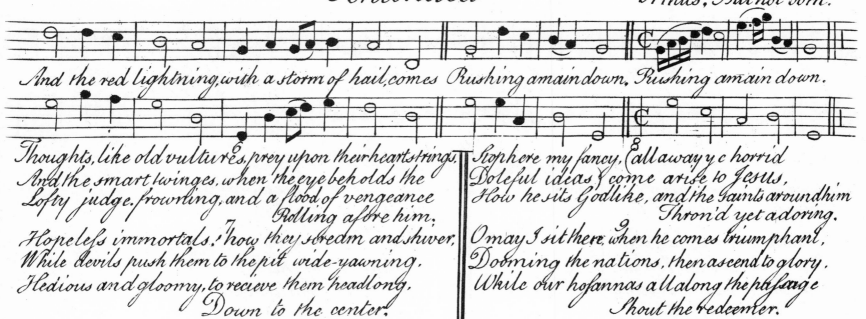

And the red lightning, with a storm of hail, comes Rushing amain down. Rushing amain down.

Thoughts, like old vultures, prey upon their heartstrings,
And the smart twinges, when the eye beholds the
Lofty judge, frowning, and a flood of vengeance
    Rolling afore him,
Hopeless immortals! how they screm and shiver,
While devils push them to the pit wide-yawning.
Hedious and gloomy, to recieve them headlong.
    Down to the center.

Stop here my fancy, (all away ye horrid
Doleful ideas) come arise to Jesus,
How he sits Godlike, and the saints around him
    Thron'd yet adoring.
O may I sit there, when he comes triumphant,
Dooming the nations, then ascend to glory.
While our hosannas all along the passage
    Shout the redeemer.

Whitefields

Come thou almighty king, Help us thy name to sing, Help us to praise.; Father all glorious, O'er all vic-

Jesus our Lord, arise,
Scatter our enemies,
And make them fall;
Let thine almighty aid,
Our sure defence be made,
Our souls on thee be staid,
Lord, hear our call.

Come holy comforter,
Thy sacred witness bear,
In this glad hour:
Thou, who almighty art,
Decend in every heart,
And ne'er from us depart,
Spirit of power.

torious, come and reign over us, Antient of days.

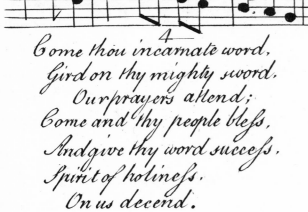

4

Come thou incarnate word,
Gird on thy mighty sword,
    Our prayers attend;
Come and thy people bless,
And give thy word success,
Spirit of holiness,
    On us decend.

5

To the great one in three,
Eternal praises be,
    Hence ever more;
Thy sov'reign majesty
May we in glory see,
And to eternity,
    Love and adore.

192 *Christmas*

While shepherds watch'd their flocks by night, All seated on the ground, The angel of the Lord came on the ground

down, And glo————————ry shone around, And glory shone around. Fear not saidhe, for

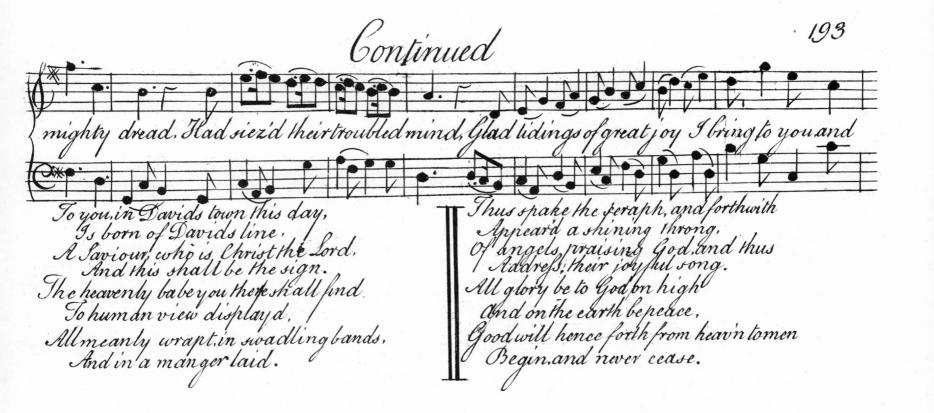

mighty dread. Had siez'd their troubled mind, Glad tidings of great joy I bring to you and

To you, in Davids town this day,
　Is born of Davids line.
A Saviour, who is Christ the Lord,
　And this shall be the sign.
The heavenly babe you there shall find,
　To human view display'd,
All meanly wrapt, in swadling bands,
　And in a manger laid.

Thus spake the seraph, and forthwith
　Appeard a shining throng,
Of angels praising God, and thus
　Addrefs, their joyful song.
All glory be to God on high
　And on the earth be peace,
Good will hence forth from heav'n to men
　Begin, and never cease.

and like a robe & like a robe, his glory wears. Great is the Lord: what tongue can frame An equal honor to his name?

The heavens are for his curtains spread,
The unfathom'd deep he makes his bed:
Clouds are his chariot, when he flies
On winged storms, a'cross the skies.
Great is the Lord; what tongue can frame
An equal honour to his name?

Great is the Lord: what tongue can frame An equal honor to his name?

Great is the Lord; what tongue can frame An equal honor to his name?

Hallelujah

Praise ye the Lord, y immortal choir, That fill the realms above; Praise him, who form'd you of his fire And feeds you w. his love.

Thou restless globe of golden light,
Whose beams create our days,
Join with the silver queen of night,
To own your borrow'd rays.

Winds, ye shall bear his name aloud,
Thro' the ethereal blue:
For when his chariot is a cloud,
He makes his wheels of you.

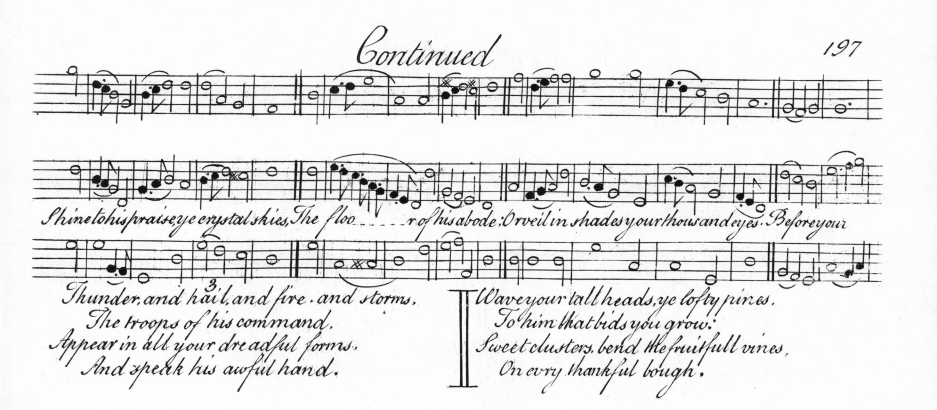

Shine to his praise, ye crystal skies, The floo——r of his abode: Or veil in shades your thousand eyes. Before your

Thunder, and hail, and fire, and storms,
The troops of his command,
Appear in all your dreadful forms,
And speak his awful hand.

Wave your tall heads, ye lofty pines,
To him that bids you grow:
Sweet clusters, bend the fruitfull vines,
On every thankful bough.

Continued

brighterGod. Hallelujah. :||: :||: :||: :||: :||: :||: Hallelujah.

Let the shrill birds his honour raise,
And climb the morning sky.
While growling beasts attempt his praise,
In hoarser harmony.

Thus while the meaner creatures sing,
Ye mortals take the sound.
Echo the glories of your King.
Thro' all the nations round.

Finis.